THE
THRIVING
CAREGIVER

Navigating Challenges with
Grace, Strength, and Prayer

By
Carolyn Wheeler

For more caregiver books, planners, journals, and free tools, visit:
www.ThrivingCaregiver.com

Acknowledgments

First and foremost, I want to thank God. Without His strength and guidance, I would not have overcome the many challenges life has brought my way. I am also deeply grateful to the countless people who have impacted my life, helping to mold me into the person I am today. To all of you, whether named here or not, please know your contributions are remembered and appreciated. A special thanks to:

- My family
- My parents
- Tammy
- Janice
- Jean
- Lucynda
- Dwight

Thank you all for your unwavering love, support, and encouragement.

Table of Contents

Message From the Author

Before we begin, I want to thank you for picking up this book. Whether you are new to caregiving or have been walking this journey for some time, I hope the insights and tools shared in these pages will support and uplift you. What makes this book even more special is that your purchase is making a difference. All proceeds from this book, as well as our accompanying Caregiver's Planner and Journal, go directly toward supporting Daisy's Place, a refuge for caregivers who need rest, resources, and community while caring for their loved ones. By using these tools, you're not only empowering yourself but also helping caregivers just like you find the support they need. Together, we can create a community of strength, compassion, and grace, thank you for being a part of that.

Chapter 1

Embracing the Journey of Caregiving

My Story:

In 2003, my youngest child, Daisy, was 17 months old. The pregnancy with her had been difficult, and the doctors had suggested she might have serious health issues, even recommending an abortion. But I had no doubt about my answer, an unwavering no.

When Daisy was born, she seemed healthy at first, but as she grew, I sensed something was wrong. I brought her to the doctors several times, but my concerns weren't taken seriously. By the time she was 17 months old, her condition had worsened so drastically that I was afraid to let her sleep, fearing she wouldn't wake up. One night, after being dismissed twice that day by doctors who said she just had croup, I rushed her to the

ER and refused to leave until they figured out what was wrong.

By the next morning, we received a devastating diagnosis, she had congestive heart failure. If she survived, she would need a heart transplant. Her ejection fraction was only 13%. We transferred her to a hospital with a pediatric cardiology department two hours away. We faced an unimaginable journey filled with experimental treatments, medical procedures, and close calls. I did all the research I could from the hospital room. I wish I had been more prepared. Was there even a way to prepare for this?

There were long nights, countless worries, and moments when I thought I would lose her. I had no car while at the hospital, but that didn't matter, I wasn't going to leave her side. I had a few friends in the area and a supportive church community at home, offering help in ways I hadn't anticipated.

When Daisy was in the ICU, the only place for me was the waiting room or to stand by her side. An older couple brought their conversion van to the hospital parking lot so I could have a place to put my things and try to sleep. Others cared for the rest of my children, ensuring their lives at home continued as normally as possible.

Of course, I put 100% of my focus on her, which was good, but in doing so, I forgot about myself.
This book is about helping you stay informed, remember self-care, and know that you do not have to do this alone.

As I reflect on that time, I realize how much caregiving transformed me first and foremost, it deepened my faith. It also taught me patience, perseverance, and the beauty of small victories, even in the darkest moments. I leaned on God more than I ever had before, and that reliance paved the way for my ongoing prayer journey, shaping the way I've navigated challenges throughout my life to this day.

Caregiving: A Gift and a Challenge

Throughout this book, we'll dive into the many aspects of caregiving, what it means to care for someone else, how to navigate the healthcare system, how to manage your loved one's legal and financial needs, and, most importantly, how to care for yourself.

You'll learn about:

- Defining Your Role as a Caregiver: Beyond just daily tasks, caregiving requires emotional, physical, and spiritual strength. We'll explore how to find balance without losing yourself in the process.

- Managing Medical Care: From understanding diagnoses to coordinating treatments, we'll walk through the essential steps to advocate for your loved one's care.

- Building a Support Network: Caregiving doesn't have to be done in isolation. We'll discuss the importance of family, friends, and community resources in lightening your load.

- Self-Care for the Caregiver: Taking care of yourself isn't just about survival, it's essential for providing the best care to your loved one. We'll explore strategies for avoiding burnout and prioritizing your well-being.

- Preparing for the Future: With caregiving comes the need to think ahead. You'll learn how to plan for future changes, whether it's in medical care, finances, or legal matters.

A Heartfelt Journey: You Are Not Alone

As you read this book, my hope is that you'll not only find the tools you need to care for your loved one and endure the journey but also feel reassured that you're making a profound difference in their life. Yes, caregiving is hard, and yes, it takes a toll. But it is also an act of love that brings moments of beauty, faith, and connection.

Speaking of love, if you haven't heard of the word "agape," now is the time to introduce it. Agape love is the highest form of love, the kind that carries you through difficult times. It's a love that gives, even when undeserved. It is filled with kindness and seeks only the best for others, without expecting anything in return. It sacrifices simply for the good of another.

For some, agape love comes naturally; for others, it may be a quality to develop along the way. Wherever you may find yourself in understanding agape love, trust that in this journey, there will be moments when agape love will be the only way through.

Yes, there will be challenges, there always are. But there will also be growth, strength, and moments of grace. We are all bound by love, the love that drives us to keep going, to push beyond what we thought possible, and to trust in a higher power that guides us through even the darkest moments.

As you begin this journey through the book, know that there are resources to support you. If you need a planner to stay organized or a journal to reflect on your caregiving days, our planners and journals are crafted with your unique caregiving needs in mind, with all proceeds going toward supporting caregivers like you. You can find them at www.thrivingcaregiver.com. Throughout this book, you'll find reflection moments and journaling prompts to help you process your experiences. Consider keeping a journal as you move through these challenges, it's not only a tool for organizing tasks but also a space for challenges, self-reflection, and renewal.

Reflection Moment:

As you start this journey, take a moment to reflect on why you became a caregiver. What brought you to this moment? How can you use this experience to grow, to find purpose, and to discover new strength? Know that you're exactly where you need to be supported by love, faith, and a community that understands.

"Commit your works to the Lord, and your thoughts will be established."
(PROVERBS 16:3, NKJV)

Prayer for Embracing the Journey of Caregiving:

Heavenly Father, I come to You with a humble heart, recognizing the weight of the caregiving journey that lies before me. Lord, I ask for Your strength when I feel weak, for Your wisdom when I feel lost, and for Your peace when I feel overwhelmed. Help me to care for my loved one with compassion, grace, and patience, reflecting Your love in everything I do. May this journey draw me closer to You, reminding me that Your presence goes before me and surrounds me even in the most difficult moments.

Give me the endurance to continue each day with a heart full of gratitude, even when the road is hard. Help me to see the beauty in small victories, and to find joy in the moments of connection and care. Father, fill me so that I may overflow with Your love, patience, and kindness. Teach me to lean on You fully, knowing that Your grace is sufficient for every challenge I face.

Guide me, Lord, in finding the right balance between caring for my loved one and caring for myself. Help me to see that in caring for myself, I am better able to serve them. Bless my efforts, and let my actions be a reflection of Your mercy and love. May this journey, though difficult, become a testimony of Your faithfulness in both my life and the life of my loved one.

I trust that You are with me every step of the way. Thank You for Your unfailing love and for the comfort of knowing I am never alone. I place my trust in You.

In Jesus' name I pray. Amen.

Notes

Chapter 2

Self-Care for the Caregiver

Caregiving can be physically and emotionally draining, making it crucial for you to prioritize your own well-being. This chapter explores the importance of self- care, recognizing signs of burnout, and practical strategies for managing stress while maintaining a healthy balance between caregiving responsibilities and personal needs. Remember, taking care of yourself is not selfish, it's essential for providing the best care for your loved one.

The Importance of Self-Care

Self-care isn't just something you squeeze in when you have time, it's essential. By caring for yourself, you're ensuring that you have the energy, patience, and emotional resilience to care for your loved one effectively. Here's why self-care matters:

- Preventing Burnout: Regular self-care practices help prevent burnout, a state of physical, emotional, and mental exhaustion that can diminish your ability to provide care.
- Maintaining Health: Prioritizing your own health through regular exercise, balanced meals, and sufficient sleep reduces the risk of illness and increases your stamina.
- Emotional Well-Being: Engaging in activities that bring you joy, and relaxation helps maintain emotional health, reducing stress and anxiety.

"Self-care is like watering a plant, you can't expect to thrive if you're running dry."

Reflection Moment:

Take a moment to consider how well you've been caring for yourself lately. Are there areas of self-care you've been neglecting?

Recognizing Caregiver Burnout

Burnout is a common issue among caregivers and can have serious consequences if left unaddressed. Here are signs to watch for:

- Physical Symptoms: Chronic fatigue, headaches, and frequent illnesses can all be signs of burnout.
- Emotional Symptoms: Feelings of overwhelm, irritability, anxiety, or depression are common emotional responses to burnout.
- Behavioral Changes: Withdrawal from social activities, neglect of personal responsibilities, or increased reliance on unhealthy habits may indicate burnout.

Recognizing these signs early allows you to take steps to manage and mitigate burnout before it escalates. It's natural to feel overwhelmed at times. Remember, experiencing these feelings doesn't mean you're failing as a caregiver, it means you're human and need support too.

Strategies for Managing Stress

Managing stress is crucial for maintaining your well-being. Here are some effective strategies:

- Mindfulness Practices: Techniques such as meditation, deep breathing exercises, and yoga can help reduce stress and improve mental clarity.

  "Even a 10-minute walk can feel like hitting the reset button on a tough day."

- Regular Exercise: Physical activity, even in small amounts, releases endorphins and helps reduce stress. As a caregiver, finding time to exercise can be a challenge, but it doesn't have to be elaborate. Try standing up and sitting down in a chair repeatedly to strengthen your legs. Walk the halls or your driveway while your loved one naps.

  Stretching throughout the day can help release tension and improve flexibility.

- Eating Right: Fast food may be quick and convenient, but planning for balanced, whole-food options can be just as easy and offers nutrients that promote sustained energy and well-being. Keep fresh fruits, nuts, and healthy snacks within reach, and consider meal prepping simple, wholesome foods to make healthier choices effortless during busy times.

• Time Management: Prioritize your tasks and delegate where possible to reduce the pressure on yourself. Creating a daily or weekly schedule can help you manage your time more effectively. "Time management isn't about doing it all, it's about knowing how to manage priorities."

• Social Connections: Maintaining relationships with friends and family provides emotional support and can help you feel less isolated.

• Spiritual Practices: Prayer, reading scripture, or attending church services can provide comfort and strength.

Incorporating these strategies into your routine can significantly improve your ability to cope with the stresses of caregiving.

Reflection Moment:

Which of these stress management strategies resonate with you? How can you incorporate them into your daily routine?

Becoming a Private Investigator WithinYourself

As a caregiver, life can present a complex mix of challenges, grief, stress, guilt, anger, and anxiety, to name just a few. It's all too easy to let these emotions take root and feel as though they define your reality. But what if you could investigate these emotions, uncover their source, and actively work to transform them?

Just as a private investigator sifts through clues to uncover the truth, you can begin to observe your own emotional responses by asking: What is this negative feeling? Where is it coming from? How could I better handle it?

Start by acknowledging the negative feeling when it arises. Do not ignore it, and do not push it away. Like an investigaror gathering evidence first, fully understand and accept what you're feeling. Whether it's anger, guilt, grief, or frustration, identify it. Then ask yourself, *What is the opposite of this emotion?* If you're unsure, use resources, ask a friend, search online, or simply reflect on it deeply. The goal is to consciously seek the positive counterpart.

Once you've identified the opposite emotion, allow it to become your focus. For example:

- If you're grieving, acknowledge that grief is a natural part of love. Yet, seek joy, even in small moments, the joy in memories, and the joy in the time you have with your loved one.
- If you're overwhelmed, take a deep breath and seek peace, a peace that reminds you you're doing your best.
- If frustration arises from daily tasks, remember that patience can transform frustration into a mindful acceptance of the moment.

Feelings vs. Words

Words are not just words. They are an expression of powerful emotions and serve as verbal tags to convey what you want and how you feel. Emotions have the power to reach deep into your soul, shifting your entire state of being. When you grieve, grief is not just a word; it's something you feel in the depths of your core. Just as deeply as you feel those challenging and sometimes negative emotions, grief, anger, and fear, you can also allow the opposite, positive emotions to penetrate your soul and transform your entire outlook.

Consider this for a moment and recognize the immense power this gives you. A quick disclaimer, certain feelings and emotions are a necessary part of the process. This is not to negate the need to feel certain ways at certain times, but rather to raise awareness of the power you hold in responding to the emotions that arise within you.

You have the power to:

- Recognize the feeling
- Analyze the feeling
- Understand why the feeling is there
- Decide to keep it or transform it into one that
  better serves the situation

By reflecting on these steps in challenging situations, you'll have the tools to respond in a way that helps instead of hinders.

Checklist: Self-Care

- ☐ Schedule regular self-care activities, such as exercise, hobbies, or relaxation time.
- ☐ Monitor your physical and emotional health for signs of burnout.
- ☐ Practice mindfulness techniques to manage stress and stay grounded.
- ☐ Prioritize balanced, whole foods in your diet to support well-being and energy.
- ☐ Create a routine with small, achievable exercises like stretching or short walks.
- ☐ Stay connected with friends, family, and support groups.
- ☐ Set reminders to ensure personal health check-ups.
- ☐ Take time to recognize and reflect on your emotions, acknowledging both positive and negative feelings as they arise.

- Practice the "investigator" technique by identifying the source of difficult emotions and consciously seeking their positive counterparts.
- Use affirming words and focus on positive emotions to shift your perspective when challenges arise.
- Journal about your caregiving journey to process experiences and celebrate small victories.

Thought Questions:

- What activities or practices help you relax and recharge?
  - Are you noticing any signs of burnout in yourself? How can you address them?
- How can you integrate more self-care into your daily routine?
- In what ways can your faith support you in prioritizing self-care?

"Do you not know that your bodies are temples of the Holy Spirit, who is in you, whom you have received from God? You are not your own; you

were bought at a price. Therefore, honor God with your bodies."

(1 CORINTHIANS 6:19-20, NKJV)

Remember, caring for yourself is a way of honoring God and the body He has given you.

Prayer for Self-Care as a Caregiver

Gracious Lord, I come to You seeking Your wisdom and guidance in this journey of caregiving. Teach me to see the importance of self-care, not as a luxury but as a necessity. Grant me the strength to set aside time to rest, to recharge, and to nourish my own body and soul, knowing that I can best care for my loved one when I also care for myself.

Lord, help me overcome the guilt or hesitation that sometimes makes self-care feel selfish. Remind me that my well-being matters to You, and that You desire for me to be renewed and refreshed.

Father, I ask that You provide me with moments of peace, no matter how chaotic the day may seem. Help me to find small ways to connect with You whether through prayer, quiet reflection, or moments of gratitude and to feel Your calming presence in each of those moments.

Thank You, Lord, for giving me the privilege of serving my loved one through this season of life. Help me trust in Your care for me as I care for them.

In Jesus' name I pray, Amen.

Notes:

Chapter 3

Defining Your Role and Responsibilities as a Caregiver

Being a caregiver is not just a role; it's a calling. It means stepping in to help someone who relies on you for support, whether it's a parent, spouse, child, or friend. The tasks involved can be overwhelming at first, but caregiving is also an opportunity to show deep care and love. Understanding your responsibilities as a caregiver is the foundation that will give you the confidence to navigate this important journey.

By the time you finish this chapter, you'll have a clearer sense of your role and practical steps to help you care for your loved one more effectively. You may even find yourself saying, "Yes, I can do this."

Personal Care

Personal care is often the most immediate need when someone requires caregiving. This can involve helping your loved one bathe, dress, or take care of their grooming. While these tasks might seem daunting at first, with time and understanding of your loved one's abilities and habits, they become manageable parts of your routine. Personal care isn't just about cleanliness; it's about preserving dignity and comfort.

Personal Care Checklist:

- ☐ Create a routine: Consistency brings comfort. Bathing, dressing, and other daily activities are easier when done at the same time each day. Routine helps your loved one feel more at ease because they know what to expect.
- ☐ Use supportive tools: Simple tools like a shower chair or safety bars can make a big difference in both safety and comfort. These tools also help you provide care more easily and confidently.

☐ Offer choices: Whenever possible, offer your loved one choices such as what to wear or when to bathe. This helps them maintain a sense of control, reducing frustration and improving cooperation.

Reflection Moment:

How are you approaching personal care tasks for your loved one? Is there anything you could do to make these tasks more comfortable and dignified for them? How can you make sure they feel respected and involved in their care?

Medical Care Management

Managing medical care can be one of the more complex parts of caregiving. It involves giving medicines at the right time, attending doctor's appointments, and keeping an eye on your loved one's health. Many caregivers feel the pressure of this responsibility but breaking it down into smaller tasks will make it easier to handle.

How to Handle Medical Care Management:

• Use a planner: A good planner and journal will be your best tools. Organized record-keeping will make caregiving manageable and efficient. Not only will it help you stay on top of daily tasks, but it will also help others assist you effectively. If something happens to you the alternative caregiver can step right in and be able to administer the best care possible.

• Track doctor visits: Log details about doctor visits, including key takeaways from the doctor and any follow-up instructions.

• Monitor medications: Keep an accurate record of medications, including dosage, timing, and any side effects to discuss with the healthcare team.

At some point, you might even impress yourself with how smoothly you're keeping track of it all, like becoming a professional multitasker who can balance a clipboard, a pill organizer, and an insightful conversation all at once.

Reflection Moment:

Are you confident in managing the medical care of your loved one? Are there any areas where you feel you could use additional support or tools? Who in your circle or community might be able to offer help when needed?

Emotional Support

Caregiving goes far beyond physical tasks. It's about providing emotional support, which can be one of the most rewarding parts of the job. Your loved one may experience a wide range of emotions, from frustration to loneliness, and being there for them can make a world of difference.

How to Provide Emotional Support:

- Listen without interrupting: Sometimes the best thing you can do is simply be there to listen. Whether your loved one is sharing fears, hopes, anger or just day-to-day thoughts, being a patient listener helps them feel heard and understood.

- Spend meaningful time together:
  Quality time strengthens your bond. Whether it's watching a favorite TV show, reading, or simply sitting in silence, these moments matter.
- Encourage social connections: Help your loved one stay connected with friends and family, even if it's just through phone calls or video chats. Connection is essential for well- being.

Reflection Moment:

How are you handling the emotional aspects of caregiving? How can you help your loved one feel more connected and supported? Are there any small changes you can make to provide more emotional comfort?

Household Management and Advocacy

Caregiving often means managing the household as well, including tasks like cooking, cleaning, and organizing bills. It can feel overwhelming, especially when added to caregiving duties, but establishing a system can help.

Household Management Tips:

- Delegate tasks: If others are willing to help, let them. This might involve asking family members to pitch in or hiring outside help for household chores.
- Set priorities: Focus on what matters most each day and let go of the less important things when needed.

Being an advocate for your loved one also means speaking up on their behalf when necessary. This could involve advocating for their care with doctors or even navigating legal issues like power of attorney or medical directives. Always remember that you are your loved one's voice when they can't speak for themselves or may not be able to make clear decisions.

Reflection Moment:

How do you feel about balancing household tasks with caregiving? What small steps could you take to make these tasks easier on yourself? Who might you ask for help to lighten the load?

"Bear one another's burdens and so fulfill the law of Christ."

(GALATIANS 6:2, NKJV)

As a caregiver, you are in a unique position to provide care and kindness to your loved one. Every action you take, no matter how small, is an expression of love and compassion. You are offering good in a way that reflects your values and faith, and it's a powerful testimony of your strength and character.

Prayer for Defining Your Role and Responsibilities as a Caregiver

Dear Lord, I come to You, recognizing the honor and responsibility of this caregiving role. You have placed me in this position for a purpose, to love and care for someone who needs my strength, patience, and kindness. As I serve in this capacity, I ask for Your guidance and support in every task, big or small. Help me to be mindful of the needs of my loved one and to act with a spirit of gentleness and grace.

Please grant me wisdom as I navigate the various aspects of caregiving. May I grow in understanding, patience, and compassion each day, finding strength in Your love when I feel weary. Let my actions reflect Your kindness and help me to carry out this work with a heart full of love.

Lord, remind me that I am not alone in this journey. Surround me with those who can help and encourage me and give me the courage to ask for help when I need it. Let me be a source of peace and comfort to my loved one, and may this journey bring us both closer to You.

In Jesus' name, I pray, Amen.

Notes:

Chapter 4
Building a Support Network

Caregiving can feel isolating at times, but it doesn't have to be a solo mission. Building a strong support network is essential not only for your well-being but also for the quality of care your loved one receives. This chapter will explore how to involve family, friends, and community resources; the benefits of joining support groups; and how to create a network that provides emotional, practical, and informational support. Remember, as a caregiver, you're not alone, help is often just a conversation away.

The Importance of Asking for Help

It's natural to hesitate to ask others for help, whether it's out of concern for burdening them or a belief that they may not have time. However, keep in mind that those around you may want to help, they simply may not know how, or they might not realize you need it. By reaching out, you open the door for others to support you in ways that can be both meaningful and manageable.

When you ask for help, you also give others the gift of being able to give of themselves, creating a sense of purpose and value in the connection. Many people find joy and fulfillment in helping others; by allowing them to share the caregiving load, you're providing them with an opportunity to experience that joy. Not asking keeps what could be a blessing to others a hidden secret.

Involving Family and Friends

Your immediate network of family and friends can be a vital source of support. Make a list of your day-to-day tasks. Determine which things can be done by others. Write them down. Show them the list. Let them help! Here's how to involve them effectively:

• Assign Specific Roles: Identify tasks that others can help with, such as running errands, providing meals, or spending time with your loved one to give you a break. Even small tasks can alleviate pressure and allow you to focus on what matters most.

- Communicate Openly: Keep your support network informed about your loved one's condition and your needs as a caregiver. Clear communication prevents misunderstandings and ensures that everyone is on the same page.
- Set Boundaries: While involving others is important, it's also crucial to set boundaries to protect your own time and energy. Be clear about what you can and cannot handle.

Navigating Family Dynamics

Caregiving often involves more than just one person. Family dynamics can play a significant role in shaping the caregiving experience, and it's not uncommon to encounter differing opinions on how care should be provided. Here's how to navigate these dynamics effectively:

- Clarify Roles: Clearly define each family member's role in caregiving to avoid misunderstandings. By setting expectations, you help reduce confusion and create a smoother experience for everyone involved.

- Encourage Open Communication: Family members may have differing opinions about care decisions. Encourage respectful dialogue where everyone's perspective can be shared. Sometimes just being heard is enough to ease tensions.

- Involve Distant Family Members: For family members who live far away, discuss ways they can contribute to caregiving. This might include helping financially, assisting with planning, or being available for emotional support during check-in calls. Focus on the Common Goal:

- Remind everyone involved that the priority is your loved one's well-being. Keeping this shared purpose at the forefront can help to bring everyone together, even during challenging times.

Reflection Moment:

Reflect on the relationships with your family members as you take on this caregiving journey. Are there areas of disagreement that need to be addressed? How can you work together as a family to prioritize your loved one's needs?

Utilizing Community Resources

Community resources can provide additional support and services that may not be available within your immediate network:

- Local Support Services: Many communities offer services such as meal delivery, transportation assistance, and respite care. Research what's available in your area and make use of these resources.
- Healthcare and Social Services: Reach out to local healthcare providers, social workers, and nonprofits that specialize in caregiving. They can offer guidance, referrals, and sometimes financial assistance.
- Educational Resources: Attend workshops or seminars on caregiving to learn new skills and stay informed about best practices.

Joining Caregiver Support Groups

Support groups offer a space to connect with others who understand the challenges of caregiving. Here's why they are beneficial:

- Emotional Support: Sharing experiences with others in similar situations can provide emotional relief and reduce feelings of isolation.
- Information Sharing: Support groups are a great place to learn from others' experiences, discover new resources, and get advice on managing specific challenges.
- Building Relationships: Developing relationships with other caregivers can create a sense of community and provide ongoing support beyond the group meetings.

Reflection Moment:

Consider how joining a support group could benefit you. What hesitations might you have about joining one, and how can you overcome them?

Checklist: Building a Support Network

- ☐ Identify family and friends who can assist with caregiving tasks.
- ☐ Communicate openly with your support network about your needs and limitations.

- ☐ Research and utilize community resources and services.
- ☐ Join a caregiver support group, either locally or online.
- ☐ Set boundaries to protect your time and energy.
- ☐ Pray for guidance in building and maintaining your support network.

Thought Questions:

- • Who in your immediate circle can you rely on for help?
- • Are there community resources you haven't yet explored that could assist you?
- • How can joining a support group enhance your caregiving experience?
- • In what ways can your faith community support you in your caregiving journey?

"Two are better than one, because they have a good return for their labor: If either of them falls down, one can helpt he other up."

(ECCLESIASTES 4:9-10, NKJV)

Remember, accepting help is not a sign of weakness but a recognition of the importance of community in our lives.

Prayer for Building a Support Network:

Heavenly Father, I come before You, asking for Your wisdom as I navigate the challenges of caregiving. I know that You did not create us to carry our burdens alone, and I thank You for placing people in my life who can help lighten the load. Lord, guide me in reaching out to family, friends, and the community for support. Give me the humility to ask for help when I need it and the discernment to know when to accept it.

Help me to build strong connections with others who can walk alongside me in this journey. Surround me with people who will encourage and uplift me, who will listen with compassion and offer assistance without judgment. I pray for the wisdom to set healthy boundaries and the strength to communicate my needs clearly and confidently.

Father, I ask that You lead me to the right resources where I can find understanding and support. May I find peace in the community of fellow caregivers, knowing that together, we can bear one another's burdens. In those moments when I feel isolated or overwhelmed, remind me of Your constant presence and love.

Thank You, Lord, for providing me with the people and resources I need to care for my loved one. I trust that You will continue to open doors for support and guidance, and I pray that through these connections, I will grow in strength and grace. In Jesus' name I pray, Amen.

Notes:

Chapter 5

Navigating Insurance and Medical Paperwork

Insurance may seem like a dry topic, but understanding it forms a foundation that can make a world of difference in caregiving. Familiarity with insurance options, from standard health plans to supplementary coverages like long-term care or accident insurance, empowers you to make informed decisions and potentially uncover benefits that ease your financial burden. And while the details may feel overwhelming, there's help available if you know where to look.

Let's dive into why insurance matters and how staying organized with paperwork can help you free up time and energy to take care of yourself, making caregiving smoother and less stressful.

Types of Insurance to Consider

Beyond health insurance, other policies may offer crucial support in certain situations:

- Cancer Insurance - Covers many cancer-related treatments, from hospital stays to specialized care.
- Accident Insurance - Provides benefits for accident-related injuries, especially helpful if your loved one is prone to falls.
- Long-Term Care Insurance - Covers services that health insurance often won't, such as in-home care or assisted living.
- Medicare and Medicaid - Government programs with significant coverage options based on age or income. Learning about these can bring valuable support to your caregiving role.

Where to Get Help with Insurance Complexities

Insurance agents, patient advocates, or state programs can provide expert guidance and help you feel more confident in navigating insurance details. You don't have to tackle this alone, these professionals are available to help every step of the way.

Staying Organized with Insurance and Medical Paperwork

Keeping insurance documents and medical records organized isn't just helpful; it's essential for managing bills, claims, and payments effectively. Knowing where each document is can give you peace of mind and a sense of control during challenging times.

Remember: Organization isn't just about paperwork. By staying organized, you're freeing up your mental space to focus on what matters most, your loved one's well-being and your own self-care. With everything in its place, you'll have time to breathe, reset, and recharge, so you can bring your best self to caregiving.

Practical Tips for Managing Medical Bills and Explanation of Benefits (EOBs)

After a hospital visit, you may receive numerous bills from various providers, alongside EOBs from your insurance company. To manage these effectively, follow these steps:

1. Read Each Document Carefully - Review each bill and EOB thoroughly. If you have questions, call the customer service number on the bill or EOB.

2. Organize by Provider - Separate bills and EOBs by provider, insurance company, or hospital, creating stacks or folders for each.

3. Match Bills to EOBs - Find the date of service and amount on each bill. Match these details to the corresponding EOB, which shows the insurance processing details. Attach them together to make tracking easier.

4. Determine Payment Status - Check if the bill is paid in full or has a remaining balance. The EOB will indicate whether insurance covered the

charge, denied it, or requires additional information.

Organize with Folders or an Accordion File:

- Paid in Full - File bills that are fully paid in a folder labeled "Paid in Full."
- Awaiting Insurance Payment - Place bills awaiting insurance processing in a "Needs Payment from Insurance" folder. Follow up with your insurance company as needed.
- Needs Payment from Me - File bills requiring your payment in a "Needs Payment from Me" folder. Once paid, move them to "Paid in Full."
- Follow Up Regularly - If a claim isn't paid within 30 days, contact your insurance company. Staying proactive prevents small issues from becoming major headaches.

Taking Care of You, Too

As a caregiver, it's easy to overlook your own needs while juggling paperwork, appointments, and daily tasks. But remember, taking care of yourself isn't just a luxury, it's a necessity. When you stay organized, you reduce the stress of not being prepared, knowing you have everything you need at your fingertips during critical moments. This clarity lets you set aside time for self-care.

• Self-Care is Supported Care - The time you spend organizing and managing these tasks directly benefits your mental health. You're creating more space to recharge, which ultimately strengthens your ability to care for your loved one.

Insurance and Financial Preparation Checklist

☐ Review each insurance policy to understand coverage, deductibles, and copayments.

☐ Organize medical paperwork, including records, statements, and policy documents, in a filing system.

☐ Confirm that all personal information is accurate with each insurance provider.

- ☐ Create a contact list with phone numbers and emails for insurance representatives, healthcare providers, and relevant support services.
- ☐ Set reminders to review and update policies annually.
- ☐ Seek assistance from an advisor, social worker, or ombudsman if you're struggling with coverage details.
- ☐ Verify that you have an emergency plan that includes necessary medical and insurance documents.

Reflection Moment

Think about the peace of mind that comes with knowing everything is organized and easily accessible. Imagine using that saved energy to recharge, be more present with your loved one, or take a well-deserved break. How would that feel?

Consider:
- How would a clearer organizational system ease your caregiving journey?

• What are your biggest challenges with insurance, and who could help you manage them?

Prayer for Clarity and Guidance in Organizing Insurance and Paperwork

Heavenly Father, I ask for Your wisdom and patience as I navigate the complexities of insurance and medical paperwork. Help me find clarity amid the confusion and confidence in making the right decisions for my loved one's care. Lord, provide me with the resources and support I need, guiding me to the people and tools that can ease this burden.

Grant me peace when the paperwork feels overwhelming and comfort in knowing that You are always with me, helping me through each challenge. Remind me to lean on You, Lord, and to trust in Your provision. Give me the strength and perseverance to continue caring for my loved one, confident in Your guidance.

In Jesus' name, I pray, Amen.

Notes:

Chapter 6

Medical Care and Treatment Planning

Navigating medical care and treatment planning for your loved one is a critical aspect of caregiving. This chapter will guide you through understanding your loved one's medical needs, working with healthcare providers to develop a treatment plan, and ensuring effective communication with medical staff. By being proactive and organized, you can help ensure that your loved one receives the best possible care while finding strength in your faith throughout this process.

Understanding Your Loved One's Medical Needs

As a caregiver, it's essential to have a comprehensive understanding of your loved one's medical conditions. This knowledge allows you to make informed decisions and advocate effectively on their behalf. Many times,

I've been in conversations with friends about their caregiving situations, and as we talked through them, we realized how many opportunities to gather more information had been missed. The best thing you can do is ask, ask, and then ask again. Of course, ask in a kind and deeply interested way, but ask.

Take time to think ahead and write down the possible questions that may arise. Some questions may always be the same, and these are worth keeping on hand. Here is a list to get you started.

There is one question you must always ask: "Can I have a copy of the doctor's report and the test results?" In my caregiving journey, if there was one question that made the most difference, it was that one. Having the medical information in your hands to review can and will help you stay fully informed about the medical direction of your loved one's care. (Don't forget to file it correctly.)

General Questions to Ask at Every Doctor's Visit

1. What is my loved one's current health status?

2. Are there any new test results or changes since our last visit?
3. What are the goals of today's appointment?
4. What changes, if any, should we make to medications, dosages, or timing?
5. What side effects should we watch for with any prescribed medications?
6. Are there any new symptoms or behaviors that we should report if they occur?
7. What lifestyle changes would you recommend (diet, exercise, sleep routines)?
8. What signs would indicate that we need to seek urgent medical care?
9. What upcoming appointments, follow-ups, or tests should we schedule?
10. Is there a care plan in place, and has it changed since the last visit?
11. What should we prioritize or focus on until the next visit?
12. Who can I contact for questions or concerns between appointments?

Specific Questions for Situational or Symptom-Related Concerns

Medication Adjustments or New Prescriptions

- How long will it take for this medication to start working?
- Are there any foods, supplements, or activities to avoid while on this medication?
- Is there a generic version of this medication that would work as effectively?
- What should we do if a dose is missed?

Pain or New Symptoms

- What might be causing this new symptom or pain?
- Are there any tests we should do to investigate this symptom further?
- What pain management options are available?
- Could this be a side effect of a current medication?

Cognitive Changes

- Have you noticed any significant changes in cognitive function or memory?
- Are there strategies or therapies to help with cognitive challenges?
- Could these changes be related to a specific condition, medication, or aging process?
- How can we best support mental sharpness and memory?

Mobility or Physical Function Changes

- What can we do to improve mobility or prevent falls?
- Are there physical therapy exercises that could help?
- Would you recommend assistive devices, such as a cane, walker, or wheelchair?
- Are there specific ways to make the home safer based on current mobility?

Chronic Illness Management

- Are there updates in treatment for this condition?
- What tests are required to monitor this condition, and how often should they be done?
- Are there complications we should be especially watchful for?
- What lifestyle changes could help improve the management of this condition?

Nutrition and Hydration

- What dietary changes would you recommend based on current health?
- Are there specific foods or nutrients that could benefit this condition?
- How can we ensure adequate hydration?
- Are there supplements that would be safe and effective?

End-of-Life Care or Palliative Needs

- What options are available for managing pain and comfort at this stage?

- Are there support services (such as hospice or palliative care) we should consider?
- What is the long-term outlook, and how should we prepare?
- How can we best support their quality of life in these circumstances?

Key areas to focus on include:

- Diagnosis Overview: Understand the specifics of your loved one's medical conditions, including symptoms, prognosis, and typical treatment options. Don't hesitate to ask healthcare providers to explain anything you don't understand.
- Medication Management: Keep a detailed list of all medications, including dosages, side effects, and interactions.
- Symptom Monitoring: Learn to recognize the signs and symptoms that indicate the condition is worsening or that immediate medical attention is needed.

And yes, you'll soon know more medical jargon than you ever thought possible, don't worry, you've got this!

Reflection Moment:

Take a moment to reflect on how understanding your loved one's medical needs empowers you as a caregiver. How does this knowledge help you provide better care and bring you more confidence in managing their well-being?

Creating a Treatment Plan with Healthcare Providers

A well-coordinated treatment plan is essential for managing your loved one's health effectively. Collaborating with healthcare providers will ensure that all aspects of care are covered.

Steps to Creating a Treatment Plan:

- Regular Appointments: Schedule consistent check-ups and specialist visits to monitor your loved one's health. Keeping track of these appointments in a planner helps ensure nothing is overlooked.

- Collaborative Approach: Work closely with doctors, nurses, and other healthcare professionals to develop a comprehensive treatment plan that addresses all aspects of care.
- Care Coordination: Ensure that all healthcare providers involved in your loved one's care are communicating with each other and that you are fully informed of any changes to the treatment plan.
- Emergency Preparedness: Develop a plan for handling medical emergencies, such as knowing when to seek emergency care and having a list of emergency contacts.

Remember, you don't have to do this alone, each healthcare professional is there to guide you, and with careful planning, you can manage this aspect of caregiving effectively.

An Example Emergency Plan

1. Gather Essential Information

- Medical Contacts: Write down contact information for primary doctors, specialists, and any other relevant healthcare providers.
- Medications List: Keep an up-to-date list of all medications, dosages, and schedules.
- Medical Conditions: List your loved one's key medical conditions, known allergies, and any other vital health details.
- Insurance and ID: Make copies of health insurance cards, IDs, and any other necessary documentation.

2. Emergency Contacts

- Designate two emergency contacts (family members, neighbors, or friends) who can help or make decisions if you're unavailable.
- Share your emergency contacts with other caregivers involved, if applicable.

3. Prepare a "Go Bag"

- Medications: Pack a few days' worth of medications in a labeled container.
- Documents: Include copies of medical information, emergency contacts, insurance details, and any advanced directives (such as a medical release form, living will, power of attorney, or healthcare proxy).
- Personal Care Items: Add items like toiletries, a change of clothes, and any personal care products.
- Comfort Items: Pack anything that may ease stress or provide comfort for your loved one, like a pillow, blanket, favorite book, or music device.

4. Plan Your Transportation

- Identify a primary and backup method of transportation (your car, a friend's vehicle, or a local transport service) to use in emergencies.
- Keep a list of local hospitals or urgent care facilities, noting the ones that accept your loved one's insurance.

5. Communicate the Plan

- Share the plan with family members, friends, or other caregivers who may be involved.
- Ensure everyone knows where to find the "Go Bag" and important documents.

6. Emergency Contact Card

- Prepare a small card listing key contacts, medical information, and any urgent care needs.
- Keep this card in your wallet or phone case and provide one for your loved one.

7. Regular Review and Updates

- Review the plan every 3-6 months to update medications, doctor information, and any other details.

Reflection Moment:

What part ofcreating a treatment plan do you find most difficult? How can you involve healthcare providers more effectively to reduce your stress? What small steps can you take to feel more confident in these decisions?

Embracing Cultural Perspectives in MedicalCare

Medical care and treatment planning can be influenced by cultural backgrounds that shape views on health, treatment preferences, family roles, and communication styles. Recognizing these perspectives can deepen trust between caregivers, loved ones, and healthcare providers, creating a compassionate and respectful environment.

Understanding Cultural Influences in Medical Care

1. Family Roles and Expectations

   Insome cultures, healthcare decisions may be a family responsibility, with particular roles assigned based on age, gender, or relationship to the care recipient. For example, the eldest family member or a designated individual may be entrusted to make health decisions. Awareness of these roles can help caregivers and medical staff approach decision- making with greater sensitivity.

2. Healthcare and Treatment Beliefs

Some cultures value traditional medicine, home remedies, or herbal treatments alongside or even in place of modern medicine. Respecting these practices and understanding their importance can help caregivers advocate for a treatment plan that aligns with their loved one's values. Open communication with healthcare providers about these preferences can foster a more tailored and inclusive approach to care.

3. Approaches to Aging and Independence

Cultural views on aging can impact caregiving and medical planning. In some cultures, aging is revered, and family caregiving is expected, while others prioritize independence and autonomy for as long as possible. Recognizing these differences can help caregivers respect their loved one's dignity and preferences during the treatment planning process.

4. Communication Styles and Decision-Making

In certain cultures, family members may collectively make health decisions, while in others, the individual's personal choice is emphasized. Understanding these dynamics allows caregivers to advocate for a care plan that is both effective and culturally respectful.

Navigating Cultural Differences in Healthcare Settings

Healthcare providers may not always be aware of cultural differences, which can lead to misunderstandings. As a caregiver, you play an essential role in bridging cultural gaps and advocating for respectful, culturally sensitive care.

Tips for Culturally Sensitive Communication:

- Express Key Beliefs: Share any relevant cultural beliefs with healthcare providers that might affect treatment preferences, dietary practices, or emotional comfort.
- Ask with Respect: Inquire if certain cultural practices can be accommodated. Even small gestures, like accommodating dietary restrictions

or allowing time for certain rituals, can make a difference.

- Promote Mutual Respect: Approach cultural differences with curiosity and empathy. This openness fosters a collaborative environment where medical staff, caregivers, and family members can work together for the loved one's best interest.

Reflection Moment:

Consider how your cultural background may shape your approach to medical care and treatment. What values or traditions are important in your caregiving routine, and how can you share these with healthcare providers to ensure culturally respectful care?

Alternative Medicine as a Complementary Approach

Inaddition to traditional medical treatments,you might consider exploring alternative therapies. These approaches can turn things around and help manage symptoms like pain, anxiety, or stress. Many times, it can also be used alongside conventional treatments but again, you must ask.

In my caregiving journey the alternative approach was used very often. Not only do I not regret moving in that direction, I am so grateful for it.

Alternative Therapies to Explore:

- Infusions
- Ozone therapy
- Thermography
- Acupuncture
- Massage therapy
- Aromatherapy
- Nutritional therapy
- Herbal supplements

Functional Medicine:

Functional medicine doctors can add to the protocol as they discuss alternative options. Remember, although it can be a replacement, alternative medicine isn't always about replacing traditional treatments, it's about enhancing your loved one's quality of life.

Reflection Moment:

Have you considered incorporating alternative therapies into your loved one's care plan? Which therapies could add to quality of life?

Effective Communication with Medical Staff

Clear and concise communication with medical staff is essential to ensuring that your loved one's needs are met. As a caregiver, your voice is a vital part of your loved one's care, and expressing yourself with kindness and respect can make a powerful difference. Medical staff are more likely to respond openly and thoroughly when approached in a calm, considerate way. This positive approach fosters collaboration, allowing you to work together for the best outcomes.

Strategies for Communicating Effectively

- Prepare for Appointments: Write down questions and concerns before each appointment. This ensures that you cover all important topics, even if time is limited or emotions are high. When you show up prepared, it demonstrates to the medical staff that you respect their time and your role as a caregiver. Remember, your calm preparation helps set a tone of mutual respect and collaboration.

- Concise Communication: Be clear and to the point when discussing your loved one's symptoms, concerns, and needs with healthcare providers. Instead of long explanations, begin with the primary concern, followed by supporting details. Practicing concise communication shows kindness and respect for the busy schedules of healthcare providers, making it easier for them to listen attentively and address your loved one's needs effectively.

- Follow-Up: After appointments or treatments, follow up with medical staff to confirm any instructions and ensure necessary actions have been taken. A friendly follow-up communicates that you're not only proactive but also grateful for their guidance and support. Approach these conversations as a collaborative opportunity, reinforcing that you're both working toward the same goal of providing the best care possible.

• Documentation: Keep a detailed record of all communications with healthcare providers, including notes from appointments and any instructions given. Organized documentation helps you feel in control and reassured, and it makes it easier to communicate clearly and confidently. This kindness to yourself, keeping everything in one place, is also a kindness to the medical staff who rely on your accurate information.

Yes, that folder full of papers may look like an encyclopedia, but you'll thank yourself for keeping it all organized!

The Importance of Kind and Persistent Communication

Effectivecommunication goes beyondsimplysharing information, it's about building trust, setting a cooperative tone, and ensuring that your loved one's needs are understood and prioritized. Approaching each conversation with kindness not only strengthens the relationship between you and the medical staff but also makes it easier for you to be heard and taken seriously. Kind and clear communication allows you to advocate confidently while creating a supportive and respectful environment that fosters better care and mutual understanding.

Reflection Moment:

How are you managing your communication with healthcare providers? What strategies could you use to make your interactions smoother and more effective?

AMA (Against Medical Advice)

There may be situations where you or your loved one feel that leaving a medical facility or refusing certain treatments is the best decision, despite medical advice to the contrary. This is referred to as leaving Against Medical Advice (AMA).

While it's important to listen to medical professionals, you have the right to seek a second opinion or discuss alternatives if you're uncomfortable with recommended treatment. However, leaving AMA can have consequences, such as voiding insurance claims, so make sure you fully understand the risks before making this decision.

Reflection Moment:

How do you feel about advocating for your loved one when difficult medical decisions arise? What challenges have you faced, and how can you approach future situations with more confidence?

"So then, my beloved brethren, let every man beswift to hear, slow to speak, slow to wrath."
JAMES 1:19 (NKJV)

Approach your interactions with medical staff with grace and clarity, remembering that you are all working towards the same goal of caring for your loved one.

Preparing for a Hospital Stay

Navigating a hospital stay can be overwhelming for both caregivers and their loved ones. While hospital staff will handle much of the medical care, your role remains essential in overseeing your loved one's comfort and ensuring that vital information is consistently communicated. Planning for a hospital stay, whether it's a scheduled procedure or an unexpected admission, can make the experience smoother and more manageable.

Consider preparing in advance to minimize stress, especially if your loved one's condition makes hospital visits more likely. Have a "go bag" ready with essentials for both you and your loved one and organize any required paperwork. Being prepared allows you to focus on supporting your loved one rather than scrambling to gather items or information at the last minute.

When talking with other caregivers, one of the most mentioned and crucial pieces of advice is this: document everything. Your planner or notebook can be your best friend in a hospital setting. If you forget your toothbrush, don't forget your planner! A little humor, perhaps, but the truth is, having everything written down keeps you grounded and prepared for what can often be a chaotic environment.

A hospital stay often means working with multiple healthcare providers, so keep a record of all important medical information on hand, including medication lists, care plans, and recent test results, nurse, and doctor's names and a log of times they came in. Clear communication with the medical team is key; don't hesitate to ask questions or voice concerns if something doesn't seem right. Your advocacy can play a significant role in ensuring that your loved one receives attentive, personalized care.

Here are a few tips to help you prepare for a hospital stay:

- Be Prepared for the Unexpected: Hospital stays can often come with unexpected situations. Make sure you're familiar with the procedures at the hospital and be ready to advocate for your loved one if necessary. Remember, you're there as part of their support team.
- Bring Comfort Items: Hospitals can feel cold and impersonal, so consider bringing a few items that bring comfort, such as a colorful blanket, a favorite book, or photos of loved ones. These items can help create a sense of familiarity and ease.

1. Stay Organized: Having all essential information in one place will make it easy to access what you need, even in stressful moments. Using a planner or notebook specifically for caregiving can help keep everything organized and reduce any additional stress.

Hospital Stay Checklist

For Your Loved One:

☐ Personal pillow or blanket (choose a colorful one to prevent mix-ups with hospital linens)

☐ Comfortable clothing and slippers or a robe

☐ Toiletries (toothbrush, toothpaste, brush, lotion, etc.)

☐ Medications and medication list (ensure the hospital has the most updated list)

☐ Favorite book, puzzle book, or other small entertainment

☐ A few comfort items (e.g., family photos or a cherished keepsake)

☐ Planner or journal to record important information, doctor visits, and changes

☐ Insurance card ID, and any relevant medical documentation

For the Caregiver:

☐ Snacks, water, and any required medications

☐ Toiletries and a change of clothes

☐ Comfortable shoes and layered clothing (hospitals can be chilly)

☐ Planner or notebook for documentation

☐ Phone charger and a list of important contacts

☐ A small bag with essentials in case of unexpected overnight stays

☐ Comfort items for yourself (e.g., a book, journal, or music)

Reflection Moment:

Consider how planning for a hospital stay could ease your mind and support your loved one's comfort and care. How can you organize these preparations to ensure that you're ready for any hospital needs, both expected and unexpected?

Prayer for Medical Care and Treatment Planning:

Heavenly Father, as I step into the role of managing my loved one's medical care, I ask for Your divine wisdom and guidance. You are the ultimate healer, and I trust in Your plan, even when the journey seems overwhelming. Please give me the strength to navigate appointments, understand diagnoses, and ask the right questions.

Grant me the clarity and patience to advocate for my loved one's health and well-being. Guide me to the best decisions regarding treatment options and help me work in harmony with healthcare providers. When I am faced with difficult choices, let Your peace be my guide, knowing that You are with us in every moment of this journey.

Lord, I also pray for discernment as we explore treatment plans, traditional medicine, and alternative therapies. Help us remain open to Your leading in each step, trusting that You are present in the hands of the caregivers, the doctors, and all those who are part of this process.

Strengthen me, Lord, so I can provide compassionate care, and remind me that I can rest in You when I feel weary. May Your grace sustain us through every challenge and help us find hope and healing in the midst of uncertainty.

Thank You for walking beside me on this path of caregiving and healing.
In Jesus' name I pray, Amen.

Notes:

Chapter 7

Managing Daily Care

Daily caregiving involves a wide range of tasks that ensure your loved one's well-being and comfort. This chapter focuses on the practical aspects of managing daily care, including personal care tasks, meal planning and nutrition, and medication management. By establishing routines and systems, you can make daily caregiving more manageable and less overwhelming, while infusing moments of grace and connection into everyday tasks.

Personal CareTasks

Personal care is an essential part of daily caregiving. This includes helping your loved one with activities such as bathing, dressing, grooming, and restroom support.

Here's how to manage these tasks effectively:

- Bathing and Grooming: Establish a regular bathing schedule and ensure all necessary toiletries and grooming tools are easily accessible. If your loved one has mobility issues, adapt the bathroom setup as needed. Use this time as an opportunity for gentle conversation or prayer, making it a peaceful experience.

- Dressing: Choose clothing that is easy to put on and take off, considering any physical limitations. Encourage your loved one to participate in dressing as much as possible to maintain their independence. Offering choices in clothing can help give them a sense of control and dignity.

  But fair warning: if your loved one decides to wear their favorite sweater for the third day in a row, it's all about picking your battles. At least they're dressed, right?

- Restroom Support: Be mindful of your loved one's bathroom needs, including any incontinence issues. Make sure the bathroom is safe and accessible, with grab bars and other necessary aids. Approach these tasks with sensitivity and respect, ensuring your loved one feels comfortable and dignified.

Reflection Moment:

How can you infuse these routine tasks with love and respect? What small changes could make the experience easier and more comfortable for both you and your loved one?

Meal Planning and Nutrition

Proper nutrition is crucial for maintaining your loved one's health. Meal planning can help ensure they receive balanced and appropriate meals. Many times, good eaters become picky and picky eaters become seemingly impossible to deal with. We all need to improve our eating habits. Nutrition is the fuel our body needs to sustain life. As a caregiver it is important to assess which battles to go up against. If your loved one is in a temporary need of care, nutrition is essential for continuing improvement. If your loved one is in a state of just needing comfort until the end, of course give them as much nutrition as possible but in my opinion, ease up on your battles.

- Nutritional Needs: Work with a nutritionist or healthcare provider to understand your loved one's dietary needs, especially if they have specific medical conditions like diabetes or heart disease. Consider incorporating foods that have special meaning or bring back fond memories for your loved one. Familiar flavors can be comforting.

- Meal Preparation: Plan and prepare meals that meet nutritional needs while also considering your loved one's food preferences. Batch cooking and meal prepping can save time and reduce stress. Involve your loved one in meal planning or simple food preparation tasks, if possible, to maintain a sense of purpose.

- Hydration: Ensure your loved one stays hydrated throughout the day by providing easy access to water and other fluids.

Think of yourself as the hydration coach, always encouraging those extra sips like a pro!

Remember, mealtime is more than just nutrition, it's an opportunity for connection and comfort. Approach each meal with patience and love, understanding that eating habits and abilities may change over time.

Reflection Moment:

How can you make mealtimes more enjoyable for both you and your loved one? What changes could you make to their diet or meal preparation process to better support their needs and preferences?

Medication Management

Managing medications is a critical aspect of caregiving, requiring caregul attention to detail.

- Medication Schedule: Create a clear and organized medication schedule that includes the name of each medication, dosage, and the time it should be taken.
- Use a planner to help you stay on track with medication times.
- Pill Organizers: Use pill organizers to sort medications by day and time, reducing the risk of missed or incorrect doses.
- Monitoring: Keep track of any side effects or changes in your loved one's condition and report these to their healthcare provider.

- Refills and Storage: Ensure that medications are refilled on time and stored safely, out of reach of children or pets.

Keeping a planner on hand helps you stay on top of health updates, like being the steady reporter for your loved one's care story.

Reflection Moment:

What strategies can you use to ensure medication management stays accurate and stress-free? How can a journal or planner help you track medications and their effects on your loved one?

Adding Humor to Caregiving

Amid the routine tasks, it's important to find moments of lightness and humor. Caregiving can be stressful, and laughter can help relieve some of that tension.

Watch old time favorite shows, get some simple joke books for kids, go through the old photos and reminisce about the funny ones and the good ole days. With all the media listening opportunities we have now you can find anything from the old radio shows of the 30s to podcasts about any topic you can think of.

- A Lighthearted Approach: When helping with personal care, adding some lighthearted humor can ease the experience. For example: *"Who knew we'd get to share fashion advice every morning? You're a trendsetter!"* This small moment of humor can brighten a potentially stressful moment.
- Mealtime Joy: During mealtime, you might say something like, *"Why shouldn't you tell an egg a joke? It might crack up."* Finding humor in everyday moments helps reduce stress for both you and your loved one.

Reflection Moment:

How can you bring a little lightness and laughter into the caregiving routine? How can humor help ease the emotional weight of caregiving for both you and your loved one?

Checklist: Managing Daily Care

- ☐ Establish a regular bathing and grooming routine for your loved one.
- ☐ Create a safe and accessible bathroom environment.
- ☐ Plan meals that meet your loved one's nutritional needs and preferences.
- ☐ Ensure your loved one stays hydrated throughout the day.
- ☐ Create a clear medication schedule and use a pill organizer.
- ☐ Monitor medication side effects and refill prescriptions on time.
- ☐ Incorporate humor and moments of lightness into daily caregiving tasks.

Thought Questions

- What daily care tasks do you find most challenging, and how can you approach them with more grace?
- How can you make mealtimes more enjoyable and stress-free?

- What strategies can help you stay organized when managing medications?
- How can humor and lightheartedness become a natural part of your caregiving routine?

"And whatever you do, whether in word or deed, do it all in the name of the Lord Jesus, giving thanks to God theFather through him."

(COLOSSIANS 3:17, NKJV)

Remember, every task, no matter how mundane, can be done with a light heart, love and grace, reflecting God's care through your actions.

Prayer for Managing Daily Care

Heavenly Father, I come before You as I take on the daily tasks of caring for my loved one. Lord, I ask for Your guidance, patience, and grace as I navigate the many responsibilities of caregiving. Help me to approach each task, whether big or small, with love and compassion, knowing that every action is a reflection of Your kindness.

Grant me strength and endurance when the days feel long and remind me that You are my source of energy and peace. Help me to be sensitive to my loved one's needs, offering them dignity and respect in all aspects of care, from personal tasks to moments of connection. Guide my hands and heart, Lord, so that I may provide the best care possible with a joyful spirit, even in the hardest moments. I also ask for Your wisdom in creating routines that not only meet the physical needs of my loved one but also foster a sense of comfort and peace. Show me how to infuse each day with joy, laughter, and moments of lightheartedness even when circumstances are challenging. Help me to find strength in You and to rely on Your grace when I feel overwhelmed or uncertain.

Thank You, Lord, for giving me the privilege of serving my loved one through this season of life.

In Jesus' name I pray, Amen.

Notes:

Chapter 8

Navigating the Healthcare System

The health care system can be complex and overwhelming, especially when caring for a loved one with medical needs. This chapter will guide you through the process of navigating hospitals, understanding patient rights, advocating for your loved one, and ensuring that they receive the best possible care. With the right knowledge and strategies, you can make informed decisions and manage your loved one's healthcare journey effectively, while relying on faith for strength along the way.

Understanding Hospital Protocols

Hospitals have specific protocols and procedures that can sometimes be confusing. Here's how to navigate them effectively:

- Admission and Discharge Procedures: Familiarize yourself with the hospital's admission and discharge process. Ensure that all necessary paperwork is completed and that you understand the discharge instructions fully.
- Visitation Rules: Understand the hospital's visitation policies, especially in critical care units, to ensure you can be there when your loved one needs you most.
- Patient Rights: Learn about your loved one's rights as a patient, including the right to informed consent, privacy, and quality care. Knowing these rights will empower you to advocate effectively.

Reflection Moment:

Take a moment to consider how understanding these protocols can empower you as a caregiver. How does this knowledge help you feel more prepared to support your loved one?

"For God has not given us a spirit of fear, but of power and of love and of a sound mind."

Remember that you have the strength and clarity to navigate these complex systems with God's help.

Ensuring Quality Care During Hospital Stays

Quality care is essential when your loved one is in the hospital. Here are steps to help ensure they receive the best possible care:

- Advocate for Your Loved One: Be present as much as possible to monitor their care and communicate with healthcare providers. If something doesn't seem right, speak up immediately and keep seeking answers until you're confident your loved one is receiving the care they need.

- Keep Detailed Notes: Document everything, including the names of healthcare providers, medications administered, and any changes in your loved one's condition. This information not only helps you track treatments but also ensures nothing is missed. In unforeseen circumstances, these details can be invaluable.

- Follow Up on Care: Regularly verify that your loved one is receiving necessary care, such as timely medications, meals, and hygiene assistance. Don't assume everything is being handled, make sure it is. From my own experience, I learned just how crucial it is to stay vigilant. During our hospital stay, I caught multiple mistakes, one of which was life-threatening. I understand that mistakes can happen, we're all human, but from that point on, I made it a priority to oversee her medication personally. I double-checked each dose, ensuring everything matched her prescribed treatment.

It's natural to feel overwhelmed in a hospital setting, but remember, you are your loved one's best advocate. Your presence and attention can make a significant difference in the quality of their care.

Reflection Moment:

What are the most challenging aspects of advocating for your loved one in the healthcare system? How can you prepare yourself to be more confident in these situations?

Advocating for Your Loved One Effectively

Advocacy is a critical part of caregiving, especially within the healthcare system. Here's how to advocate effectively:

- Ask Questions: Don't hesitate to ask questions about your loved one's care. If something is unclear, ask for clarification until you fully understand. Don't feel bad to continue asking questions until you are completely clear about the situation.

- Be Assertive, Not Aggressive: Approach healthcare providers with respect, but be firm in advocating for your loved one's needs. Stay calm and focused, even in stressful situations.

- Know When to Escalate: If your concerns are not being addressed, don't hesitate to escalate the issue to a higher authority, such as a hospital administrator or patient advocate.

Reflection Moment:

How do you feel about advocating for your loved one in the healthcare system? What challenges have you faced, and how can you approach future situations with more confidence?

"Speak up for those who cannot speak for themselves, for the rights of all who are destitute." (PROVERBS 31:8, NKJV)

Your role as an advocate is a reflection of God's call to care for those in need.

Checklist: Navigating the Healthcare System

- ☐ Familiarize yourself with hospital admission and discharge procedures.
- ☐ Understand visitation rules and patient rights.

- Be present and advocate for your loved one's needs during hospital stays.
- Keep detailed notes of all interactions with healthcare providers.
- Ask questions and escalate concerns if necessary.

Thought Questions:

- Do you fully understand the hospital protocols and your loved one's rights as a patient? How can you be more proactive in ensuring quality care during hospital stays?
- Are you confident in advocating for your loved one, or do you need to learn more about your rights and options?
- How does your faith guide you in making medical decisions for your loved one?

"Let your speech always be gracious, seasoned with salt, so that you may know how you ought to answer each person."

(COLOSSIANS 4:6, NKJV)

Prayer for Navigating the Healthcare System:

Dear Lord, I come before You today seeking Your wisdom and guidance as I navigate the healthcare system on behalf of my loved one. The journey through hospital visits, medical appointments, and treatments can feel overwhelming, but I trust that You are with me in every step. Help me to be an advocate with strength and clarity, to communicate effectively with doctors and caregivers, and to ask the right questions for my loved one's well-being.

Grant me the patience and discernment to understand the complexities of medical care. When I feel lost or confused, remind me that You are my source of peace and understanding. Give me the courage to speak up when necessary and to always seek the best for my loved one. Lord, I also ask that You give me the grace to approach every healthcare worker with kindness and respect. Help me to build positive relationships with those who are caring for my loved one, and may they be instruments of Your healing. Guide their hands and hearts, Lord, so that my loved one may receive the best care possible.

Thank You for being my constant support, for Your love that never fails, and for giving me the strength to continue this journey. In Jesus' name I pray, Amen.

Technology in Caregiving: Enhancing Support at Every Step

Technology can be an invaluable tool in caregiving, assisting you in both healthcare settings and at home. From telehealth to medication reminders, using the right technology can simplify care tasks, keep you connected to medical professionals, and provide peace of mind. This section explores practical technology options that can enhance your caregiving journey.

Practical Uses of Technology in Caregiving

- Telehealth Services: Telehealth offers a convenient way to attend medical appointments, especially if frequent visits are challenging. With virtual consultations, you can connect with healthcare providers from home, review treatments, and ask questions without needing to travel. Preparing questions beforehand, just as you would for an in-person appointment, can help you get the most from these visits.

- Health Monitoring Devices: Devices such as blood pressure monitors, glucose meters, and oxygen trackers can help you keep track of your loved one's vital signs. Many devices sync with mobile apps, making it easy to log and share readings with healthcare providers. This can be especially useful for monitoring ongoing conditions and recognizing changes early.

- Home Monitoring Systems: Home monitoring systems can provide alerts if your loved one needs immediate attention, such as if they experience a fall. This can be particularly helpful for caregivers who are not always on-site. Some systems also have GPS capabilities for loved ones who may wander, offering an added layer of safety.

Using Technology at Home

In addition to healthcare settings, these technology tools can enhance your caregiving at home, making daily care more manageable and providing the structure needed for effective at-home treatment planning, as covered in Chapter 9. Consider incorporating tools that fit your loved one's needs and comfort levels, keeping in mind that even simple technology can provide big benefits for you both.

Reflection Moment:

- Which technology options could streamline your caregiving responsibilities and improve your loved one's safety?

- How comfortable are you with using digital tools in caregiving? What support do you need to make the most of these resources?

Notes:

Chapter 9

Medical Care and Treatment Planning at Home

Navigating medical care and treatment planning at home is a critical part of caregiving. This chapter offers guidance on understanding your loved one's medical needs, working with healthcare providers to create a tailored treatment plan, and establishing a system that promotes clear communication. By staying proactive and organized, you can ensure quality care at home while drawing strength from your faith.

Understanding Your Loved One's MedicalNeeds

As a caregiver, having a well-rounded understanding of your loved one's medical conditions helps you make informed decisions and advocate confidently. Here are key steps to building that knowledge:

- Diagnosis Overview: Understand the full scope of your loved one's diagnosis, including symptoms, prognosis, and treatment options. Don't hesitate to ask doctors to clarify any questions you have. If time is tight during appointments, request follow-up support from a nurse or healthcare coordinator who can provide further explanations. Familiarize yourself with common symptoms to watch for and know when to seek further medical support.
- Medication Management: Track all medications, noting dosages, potential side effects, and interactions. Keeping an organized list in a Caregiver's Planner can simplify this process, ensuring nothing is overlooked.
- Symptom Monitoring: Recognize key signs and symptoms that signal a change in your loved one's condition. Identifying these early can help you act quickly, ensuring timely medical intervention.

Reflection Moment:

Consider how a deeper understanding of your loved one's needs empowers you as a caregiver. How does this knowledge help you provide better care?

Collaborating on a Treatment Plan withHealthcare Providers

An effective treatment plan requires collaboration with healthcare providers to ensure your loved one's specific needs are met. Here's how to approach this process:

- Scheduled Appointments: Regular check-ups are vital to monitor health changes. Use a planner to track appointments, follow-ups, and any specialized care visits to stay organized and informed.
- Collaborative Approach: Partner closely with doctors, nurses, and other professionals involved in your loved one's care. Ask about what to expect at each stage and discuss ways to handle foreseeable challenges.
- Coordinating Care: When multiple providers are involved, ensure that each one communicates

with the others. Request that any changes to the treatment plan be shared with you promptly so you can stay up to date.

- Emergency Preparedness:

    Develop a straightforward plan for emergencies, including when to seek urgent care, whom to contact, and immediate steps to take. Having this plan ready can bring peace of mind and help you feel prepared.

Remember, you're not alone, healthcare professionals are there to support and guide you. With a solid plan in place, you can manage home care with confidence and care.

Reflection Moment:

How are you managing the coordination of medical care? Are there tools or systems that could streamline this process for you?

Setting Up a Home for Home Care

Creating a safe, organized, and comfortable environment is key to successful home care. Setting up your home taking medical needs into consideration, can make caregiving tasks easier and provide a reassuring space for your loved one. Here are some guidelines to help you get started:

1. Determine Equipment Needs First

    Before making any adjustments, consult with healthcare providers to identify the specific equipment needed for your loved one's care, like a hospital bed or potty chair.

2. Designate a Care Area

    Identify a primary space for caregiving activities with easy access, sufficient lighting, and room for mobility aids.

3. Organize Medical Supplies and Equipment

    Use labeled bins or shelves to organize medical supplies and track items to prevent shortages.

4. Prioritize Safety

    Install grab bars, non-slip mats, and safety devices like bed alarms to ensure a secure environment.

5. Establish a Communication Station
   Create a designated spot for caregiver notes, medical records, and important contact information.
6. Create a Comforting Atmosphere
   Personalize the care area with familiar items to provide a peaceful and comforting environment.
7. Adjust for Accessibility and Ease of Movement
   Ensure the space is wheelchair-friendly and that commonly used items are within easy reach.

Checklist: Medical Care, Treatment Planning, and Home Setup

☐ Compile a Detailed Health Summary

☐ Determine Equipment Needs

☐ Organize a Primary Care Area

☐ Schedule Regular Medical Appointments

☐ Collaborate on a Treatment Plan

☐ Establish a Communication Station

☐ Develop an Emergency Plan

☐ Monitor Symptoms and Changes

☐ Verify Regular Care Needs

☐ Maintain Safety Measures

Thought Questions:

- Do you fully understand your loved one's medical conditions and treatment options?
- How can you improve communication with healthcare providers?
- Are there any gaps in your loved one's current treatment plan that need to be addressed?
- How does your faith guide you in making medical decisions for your loved one?

"Fear not, for I am with you; Be not dismayed, for I am your God. I will strengthen you, yes, I will help you, I will uphold you with My righteous right hand." (ISAIAH 41:10, NKJV)

Prayer for Medical Care and Treatment Planning

Heavenly Father, I come to You seeking guidance, wisdom, and strength as I navigate the medical care and treatment of my loved one. In times of uncertainty, help me trust in Your plan, knowing that You are the ultimate healer. Grant me clarity as I communicate with doctors, discernment as I make decisions, and patience as I care for my loved one's physical needs.

Please be with the healthcare professionals, guiding their hands and minds to provide the best care possible. Help me find peace in the midst of medical challenges, remembering that I am never alone, for You are with me. Calm my anxieties when faced with difficult decisions and remind me to place my trust in Your healing power. Allow Your love to flow through my hands and heart as I administer care, making me an instrument of Your peace.

Give me strength for the days ahead, Lord. Allow me to see the blessings that come, even in the most trying times, and remind me of Your constant presence in every step of this journey. Surround my loved one with Your protective love, comforting them and restoring their health according to Your will.

In Jesus' name, I pray, Amen.

Notes:

Chapter 10

Legal and Financial Preparations

Stepping into the role of caregiver involves more than daily tasks; it requires careful planning to safeguard your loved one's legal and financial well-being. Preparing these essential documents not only protects their interests but also empowers you to make informed decisions when it matters most. In this chapter, we'll walk through the fundamental steps for getting organized, including establishing power of attorney, setting up living wills, managing finances, and planning for long-term care costs.

A Note on Legal Advice

This guide offers a general overview of the steps involved in legal and financial preparations, but it is not a substitute for professional legal counsel. I am not a lawyer, nor do I have the authority to provide legal advice. If you need guidance specific to your situation, please consult a qualified legal professional who can help you navigate these important details.

The Importance of Legal Documents

When caring for a loved one with medical needs, having the right legal documents in place is not just recommended, it's essential. These documents ensure that your loved one's wishes are respected and that you have the legal authority to act on their behalf, especially when it comes to making critical decisions about their healthcare and finances.

Key Documents Every Caregiver Should Have:

- Power of Attorney (POA): This legal document grants you authority to make financial decisions on behalf of your loved one.
- Healthcare Proxy: This document allows you to make medical decisions if your loved one becomes unable to do so. It's essential to have conversations ahead of time about their

preferences so you can advocate for them confidently.

- Living Will: A living will specify your loved one's wishes regarding life-sustaining treatments, such as whether they want to be placed on a ventilator or receive artificial nutrition.

- Advance Healthcare Directives: These documents outline your loved one's wishes for medical treatment and appoint someone to carry them out.

- HIPAA Authorization: The Health Insurance Portability and Accountability Act (HIPAA) limits access to medical information without consent. Having a HIPAA authorization in place ensures that you can access your loved one's medical documents, procedures, and any information you might need to support their care effectively.

Reflection Moment:

Take a moment to think about how these documents could provide peace of mind for both you and your loved one. How does being prepared, help you feel more confident in your role as a caregiver? And, let's be honest, doesn't having a plan just feel like a win?

Financial Management for Caregivers

Managing your loved one's finances can be a daunting task, especially when they are no longer able to do so themselves. As a caregiver, it's important to create a solid financial plan that takes into account both short-term and long-term needs.

Steps for Financial Management:

- Create a Budget: A budget is a practical tool for keeping track of daily living expenses, medical costs, and additional caregiving expenses like transportation, in-home care, or specialized equipment.
- Monitor Accounts: Regularly check your loved one's bank accounts, investments, and retirement funds. Make sure bills are paid on time and look for any unusual transactions, which can be a sign of fraud or misuse.
- Understand Insurance Coverage: Review your loved one's health insurance policies,

including Medicare, Medicaid, and private insurance, to understand what's covered and what isn't.

"Handling finances might feel like juggling elephants, unless you're one of those people who actually loves numbers. If not, let's thank God for the people who do, and don't hesitate to reach out to find one!"

Planning for Long-Term Care

Long-term care may be necessary for chronic illnesses or disabilities. Without preparation, it can quickly become overwhelming. Fortunately, there are ways to plan for and manage these costs.

Steps to Plan for Long-Term Care:

- Evaluate Care Options: The type of care your loved one needs will greatly impact costs. Research options such as in-home care, assisted living facilities, nursing homes, and hospice care.
- Consider Costs: Long-term care can be expensive, with nursing homes costing several

thousand dollars per month. Explore what insurance covers and determine if your loved one qualifies for government programs like Medicaid.

- Explore Financial Assistance: Veterans may be entitled to benefits through the VA, such as the Aid and Attendance benefit, which helps pay for long-term care.
- Update Your Plan Regularly: Caregiving needs can change over time, so it's important to revisit legal and financial arrangements to ensure they still serve your loved one's best interests.

Checklist: Legal and Financial Preparations

☐ Obtain and review all necessary legal documents:

☐ Power of Attorney (POA)

☐ Healthcare Proxy

☐ Living Will

☐ Advance Healthcare Directives

☐ HIPAA Authorization to ensure access to your loved one's medical information.

☐ Create and maintain a budget for caregiving and medical expenses.

☐ Monitor financial accounts and ensure all bills are paid on time.

☐ Understand insurance coverage and update policies as needed.

☐ Plan for long-term care costs and explore financial assistance options.

Reflection Moments:

• What steps have you already taken to prepare for legal and financial caregiving responsibilities? What's the next step you can take to feel even more prepared?

• Are there areas of legal or financial management where you feel uncertain? Who can you ask for help, and what resources might guide you?

• How are you balancing the emotional weight of managing your loved one's finances with your own well-being?

• When you look at the future, how do you feel about planning for long-term care needs?

• What resources can you gather now to help you feel more prepared later?

- Look back on how far you've come in managing these aspects of caregiving. You've taken on a lot, and you're making progress, give yourself credit for that.

"Commit your works to the Lord, and your thoughts will be established."
(PROVERBS 16:3, NKJV)

Look back on how far you've come in managing these aspects of caregiving. You've taken on a lot, and you're making progress, give yourself credit for that.

A Thought to Reflect On

Each step you take toward managing legal and financial responsibilities brings peace of mind and reinforces your commitment to your loved one's well-being. Recognize your progress and lean on trusted resources when needed. As you continue this journey, remember that every small effort contributes to building a foundation of stability, care, and compassion for the future.

Prayer for Legal and Financial Preparations:

Heavenly Father, I come before You, acknowledging the weight of the responsibilities I hold. As I step into the world of legal and financial preparations for my loved one, I ask for Your divine wisdom. Guide me in making decisions that honor their needs and bring peace to our situation. Help me to understand the details of legal documents, financial management, and long-term care planning. I trust that You will lead me to the right resources and people who can assist me.

Lord, in moments of uncertainty, calm my heart and remind me that You are sovereign over all circumstances. I pray for clarity as I manage finances and ensure that all legal matters are in order. Please grant me the strength to handle these tasks with diligence, knowing that You walk beside me in every step.

Thank You for providing for our needs and for the resources You place before us. May my efforts be blessed, and may Your wisdom be reflected in every decision I make. In Jesus' name I pray, Amen.

Notes:

Chapter 11

Preparing for the Future

Caregiving often involves anticipating changes and making difficult decisions about the future. Whether planning for potential health declines, understanding end-of-life care options, or ensuring that all necessary legal preparations are in place, this chapter will guide you through the essential steps to prepare for what lies ahead. By planning now, you can reduce stress and ensure that your loved one's wishes are honored, all while finding strength and guidance in your faith.

Anticipating Changes in Health

As your loved one's condition progresses, their needs may change, requiring adjustments to the care plan. Here's how to anticipate and prepare for these changes:

- Regular Health Assessments: Schedule regular check-ups to monitor your loved one's condition and adjust care plans as necessary.

Staying ahead of health changes can reduce the risk of unexpected crises.

- Adaptation of Care: Be prepared to modify the care environment, such as making the home more accessible or hiring additional help as needed. Consider changes in mobility, vision, or cognitive ability when assessing potential adjustments.
- Proactive Discussions: Have open conversations with your loved one about potential health changes and their preferences for care as their condition evolves. Discussing these matters early allows for clear understanding and peace of mind.

Reflection Moment:

Take a moment to consider how being proactive about potential health changes can provide peace of mind. How does planning ahead align with your faith's teachings about stewardship and care?

"You will keep himin perfect peace, whose mind is stayed on You, because he trusts in You."
(ISAIAH 26:3, NKJV)

Understanding End-of-Life Care Options

End-of-life care is a difficult but necessary topic to discuss. Understanding the options available can help you and your loved one make informed decisions:

• Hospice Care: Hospice provides compassionate care for those nearing the end of life, focusing on comfort rather than curative treatment. It includes medical care, pain management, and emotional support for both the patient and family.

• Palliative Care: Similar to hospice, palliative care can be provided at any stage of a serious illness and focuses on improving quality of life by managing symptoms and stress.

• Advance Directives: Ensure that your loved one's wishes for end-of-life care are documented in advance directives, including whether they want life-sustaining treatments. These documents provide clarity in difficult moments and ensure that their preferences are respected.

Discussing end-of-life care can be emotionally challenging. Remember, these conversations, while difficult, are acts of love and respect for your loved one's wishes.

Legal and Financial Preparations for theFuture

In addition to end-of-life care, there are important legal and financial steps that should be taken to prepare for the future:

- Wills and Trusts: Ensure that your loved one's assets are distributed according to their wishes by having an up-to-date will or trust in place. This legal foundation provides security and reduces potential conflict.

- Funeral Planning: Discuss and document your loved one's wishes regarding funeral arrangements, including whether they prefer burial or cremation, and any specific desires for the service.

- Power of Attorney: If not already in place, ensure that you or another trusted individual has the legal authority to make decisions on your loved one's behalf if they become unable to do so.

Reflection Moment:

Consider how having these legal and financial matters in order can provide a sense of peace and allow you to focus on what truly matters and spending quality time with your loved one.

Checklist: Preparing for the Future

- ☐ Schedule regular health assessments to monitor changes in your loved one's condition.
- ☐ Discuss and document end-of-life care preferences with your loved one.
- ☐ Ensure that all necessary legal documents, such as wills, trusts, and advance directives, are in place.
- ☐ Review and update funeral plans according to your loved one's wishes.

☐ Establish or review power of attorney to ensure you have the authority to make necessary decisions.

Thought Questions:

- Have you and your loved one discussed their preferences for end-of-life care?
- How can you approach this conversation with compassion and clarity?
- Are there any legal or financial preparations that still need to be completed?
- How can you ensure that your loved one's wishes are respected as their condition changes?
- In what ways can your faith provide comfort and guidance as you plan for the future?

"Trust in the Lord with all your heart and lean not on your own understanding; in all your ways submit to Him, and He will make your paths straight."

(PROVERBS 3:5-6, NKJV)

As you prepare for the future, remember that you can find strength and guidance in your faith. Trust that God will provide wisdom as you navigate these challenging decisions.

Prayer for Preparing for the Future:

Heavenly Father, as I look ahead and prepare for the changes that may come in this caregiving journey, I seek Your wisdom and peace. Help me navigate the uncertainties of the future with confidence, knowing that You are with me in every decision. Guide me in making choices that honor my loved one's needs and protect their well-being. Grant me discernment in planning for their care, legal matters, and financial responsibilities.

Lord, in moments of fear or doubt, remind me that You hold the future in Your hands. Help me to trust in Your perfect plan and to seek Your guidance every step of the way. Let my heart be at peace, knowing that You provide for us in all circumstances, and that nothing is too great for Your love and grace.

I also ask for the strength to have difficult conversations with my loved one about end-of-life care, trusting that these discussions will bring clarity and peace to us both. May I rely on Your presence in every decision, and may You provide the grace to carry through each step with wisdom and compassion.

In Jesus' name I pray, Amen.

Notes:

Chapter 12

Transitioning from Caregiving

The role of a caregiver is both rewarding and challenging, but there may come a time when your caregiving duties come to an end. Whether due to your loved one's recovery, a transition to professional care, or their passing, the end of caregiving can bring a mix of emotions. This chapter will guide you through the process of transitioning out of caregiving, handling grief, and finding new purpose in life after caregiving, all while maintaining your faith and spiritual connection.

Handling the Transition

The transition from caregiving can be a significant adjustment, often leaving caregivers feeling a sense of loss or uncertainty in purpose. Whether the caregiving process came on suddenly and ended just as quickly, or evolved into a long-term journey, no matter how prepared you may feel, when the time comes, it is often

different than expected, and you may not feel fully prepared. The absence of your loved one's companionship, the roles they played in your life and family, and the daily rhythms of caregiving can create a new emptiness. Here's how to navigate this change:

• Gradual Transition While Staying Involved: If your loved one transitions to professional care, easing out of your hands-on caregiving role can be a big adjustment. Your role is still essential, even if others are now involved in their day-to-day care. It's equally important to ensure they're receiving quality care by staying connected and engaged in their well-being. Allow yourself to focus on your new balance, knowing that you are still supporting your loved one while also taking care of yourself. Visit regularly, stay involved in care decisions, and remember that taking much-needed time for yourself doesn't mean you are letting go of your caregiving role.

- Acknowledge Your Feelings: It's normal to experience a range of emotions, including relief, sadness, and even guilt. Allow yourself to feel these emotions and understand that they are a natural part of the transition. Embrace the positive and let go of the negative. Missing the things your loved one did, their companionship, and the ways they filled your life may be painful, and it's okay to grieve these changes.

- It's Okay to Live Again: Moving forward doesn't diminish your loved one's importance or make their memory any less meaningful. It's okay to live again and to move on, this doesn't make their memory in vain. You are here, and as long as you are here, you deserve to live and embrace a new flow in life. Focus on the positive, honoring their legacy while creating your own new direction.

- Seek Closure, Now and for the Future: If your caregiving journey ends due to your loved one's passing, finding ways to say goodbye and honor their memory can help you find closure in the present, as well as in the future. This might involve participating in their funeral planning, creating a memorial, or simply spending time reflecting on your experiences together. It's important to create ways to remember them without guilt and allow yourself peace when you think of their memory.

Reflection Moment:

Take a moment to consider how this transition reflects God's plan for different seasons in our lives. How can you find peace in this change?

"To everything there is a season, and a time to every purpose under the heaven."
(ECCLESIASTES 3:1, NKJV)

Coping with Grief and Loss

If your caregiving role ends due to the passing of your loved one, grief and loss can be overwhelming. Here's how to cope:

- Allow Yourself to Grieve: Grieving is a deeply personal process, and there's no right or wrong way to do it. Give yourself permission to mourn and take the time you need to heal.

- Seek Support: Don't go through grief alone. Reach out to friends, family, or a grief counselor for support. Consider joining a bereavement support group where you can share your experiences with others who understand what you're going through.
- Honor Your Loved One: Find ways to keep your loved one's memory alive, whether through creating a memory book, planting a tree, donating to a cause in their name, or participating in activities they enjoyed. Honoring their memory can be a healing process.

Remember, grief is a journey, and it's important to be patient with yourself as you navigate this challenging time. You will go through phases. Do some research on the phases so that in recognition of them you will feel a comfort and a sense of normal in the process. Share with others, find those who have been there and let your faith be a source of comfort and strength during this period.

Finding a New Purpose

After caregiving ends, many people struggle with a sense of purposelessness. Finding new meaning and direction in life is an essential part of moving forward:

- Reevaluate Your Goals: Take time to reflect on what's next for you. What are your passions? What goals have you put on hold while caregiving? Consider pursuing hobbies, volunteering, or even a new career path that brings you fulfillment.
- Reconnect with Yourself: Caregiving often requires putting others' needs first. Now is the time to focus on yourself, reconnect with old friends, indulge in activities you enjoy, and take care of your physical and mental well-being.
- Explore New Opportunities: Look for new opportunities to give back or contribute to your community. Many former caregivers find purpose in church, volunteering, mentoring, or

advocacy work related to caregiving or healthcare.

Reflection Moment:

Consider how yourcaregiving experience has shaped you. How can you use the skills and compassion you've developed to serve others in new ways?

Checklist: Transitioning from Caregiving

- ☐ Acknowledge and process your emotions as you transition out of caregiving.
- ☐ Seek closure through memorials, reflection, or gradual transition.
- ☐ Allow yourself to grieve and seek support from friends, family, or support groups.
- ☐ Explore new opportunities and goals that bring you fulfillment and purpose.
- ☐ Reconnect with yourself and prioritize your well-being.

Thought Questions:

- How do you feel about the end of your caregiving journey?
- What new opportunities or goals are you interested in pursuing?
- How can you honor the memory of your loved one while moving forward?
- In what ways has your faith supported you through your caregiving journey, and how can it guide you now?

"For I know the plans I have for you," declares the Lord, "plans to prosper you and not to harm you, plans to give you hope and a future."

(JEREMIAH 29:11, NKJV) God has plans. Trust in His guidance as you move forward.

Prayer for Transitioning from Caregiving:

Dear Lord, I come to You in this time of transition, seeking Your strength and comfort. As the role of caregiving shifts or comes to an end, I ask for peace in my heart and the courage to embrace this new chapter of my life. Help me to honor the memories of the journey, whether filled with challenges or blessings, and to trust in Your guidance as I move forward.

Lord, I lift up my grief, my sense of loss, and the uncertainty that may follow this transition. I ask You to fill the space left behind with Your love and purpose. May I find new meaning and direction, guided by Your wisdom and grace. Help me also to celebrate the love and care I provided, knowing that I did so through Your strength and with Your help.

As I move forward, allow me to discover new opportunities for growth, healing, and service. I trust that You will walk with me, as You have through every step of my caregiving journey. May Your peace be with me, and may Your love sustain me as I embrace the future You have prepared.

 In Jesus' name I pray, Amen.

Notes:

Chapter 13

Celebrating Your Caregiving Legacy and Building Community

A Legacy of Care

As caregivers, you've not only traveled a difficult and rewarding journey but also created a legacy of love, patience, and resilience. This legacy is not merely defined by the day-to-day care you provided but by the example, inspiration, and guidance you now offer to others. Whether you realize it or not, your journey has become a beacon of strength for those around you, especially those who may one day walk a similar path.

Celebrating the Legacy of Your Loved One

Your loved one's life has undoubtedly left a lasting mark on you and others around them. Reflecting on

145

their legacy provides a unique opportunity to cherish and honor the values, lessons, and love they shared with you. From their unique quirks and memorable moments to the values they held dear, these elements contribute to a legacy that continues to inspire and uplift those left behind. In celebrating their life, you recognize the ways they influenced your journey as a caregiver, helped shape your character, and left a lasting impact on your heart.

Take time to remember the stories that brought laughter and light, the resilience they demonstrated in the face of challenges, and the love they poured into relationships. This legacy isn't just for you to hold onto but is a gift that you can share with family, friends, and even future generations. By keeping their spirit alive through memories, stories, and meaningful traditions, you continue to honor the impact they've had on the world.

Ways to Celebrate Their Legacy:

- Create a Memory Book or Scrapbook:
  Gather photos, favorite sayings, or stories that

capture the essence of your loved one's life. This can become a cherished keepsake for you and your family.

- Share Stories with Others: Whether it's through a family gathering, social media, or a written memoir, sharing their story keeps their memory alive and allows others to see the impact they've made.
- Continue Their Traditions: Embrace and pass on the traditions they held dear, from small daily routines to holiday customs, as a way to feel connected to them.
- Find Small Ways to Reflect Their Values: Engage in acts of kindness, generosity, or faith that embody what they believed in, allowing their influence to continue in the world.

Celebrating Wins, Goals, and Milestones

Take time to honor the progress you and your loved one made together. Even small victories, like mastering a routine, finding a moment of joy, or learning something new, are worth celebrating. Your caregiving milestones symbolize resilience, dedication, and growth. Reflecting on these accomplishments is not only an acknowledgment of hard work but a way to recharge your spirit and recognize your journey's profound impact.

Reflection Moment:

"Celebrate each step, each win, and each lesson learned. You've traveled far, and each moment has shaped you. Embrace the joy of your journey and the legacy it leaves behind, honoring both your strength and the life of your loved one."

Creating Connections and Building Community

Now that you've gained invaluable experience, it important enough to mention again, consider the gift of sharing it with others. Building connections in caregiving communities, whether through support groups, volunteer work, or simply being a friend to someone in a similar role, fosters a powerful sense of unity and understanding. Your story, experiences, and insights can offer hope and guidance to others, making their journey less daunting.

Thought Exercise:

Reflect on the impact you've made on those around you. How can you continue to share your legacy and that of your loved one, offering guidance to those who might need a supportive voice?

Checklist: Ways to Share and Celebrate Your Legacy

☐ Share Your Story: Consider sharing your experiences in a caregiver group or one on one. Your insights may encourage someone else.

☐ Celebrate Your Loved One's Life: Find ways to honor and remember the legacy of your loved one, perhaps through a memorial, a written tribute, or even small daily acts that reflect their values.

☐ Mentor New Caregivers: Many are beginning the caregiving journey just as you did. Offering mentorship can bring a sense of purpose and fulfillment.

- ☐ Volunteer for Caregiver Organizations: Your experience can be invaluable to organizations supporting caregivers.
- ☐ Recognize Your Growth: Create a personal journal of milestones and reflections that celebrates your journey and its impact on others.

Reflection:

By embracing your experiences and celebrating each step, you become both a model and a source of strength for others. Let this legacy be one of courage, compassion, and community, a lasting testament to the love and resilience you've demonstrated along the way.

Prayer of Gratitude and Purpose:

"Lord, thank You for guiding me through my caregiving journey and shaping me into who I am today. I pray for continued strength to offer support to others who need it, and for the wisdom to celebrate each moment as a part of Your greater plan. May my experiences serve as encouragement to those who need hope. In Jesus' name, Amen."

"As each one has received a gift, minister it to one another, as good stewards of the manifold grace of God."
1PETER 4:10 (NKJV)

Notes:

Chapter 14

Gratitude in Every Season of Life

Prayer is not just a refuge for hard times; it is an ongoing conversation with God, deeply rooted in gratitude and trust.

Philippians 4:6-7 reminds us of the importance of thanksgiving in prayer:

"Be anxious for nothing, but in everything by prayer and supplication, with thanksgiving, let your requests be made known to God; and the peace of God, which surpasses all understanding, will guard your hears and minds through Christ Jesus.

These verses remind us that we can approach God with everything, our joys, burdens, and uncertainties, always offering thanks in the process. When we do this, we open our hearts to God's peace, which far exceeds what we can comprehend.

In every season of life, whether in abundance or in lack, joy or sorrow, there is always something to be grateful for. Gratitude helps us lift our eyes beyond the immediate challenges and shifts our focus toward God's unwavering goodness. Prayer is our opportunity to recognize His hand in all things, even when we don't see the full picture. It is through constant communion with Him, acknowledging His role in our lives, that we find the strength to endure, the grace to forgive, and the peace to keep moving forward.

Gratitude in prayer also fosters a sense of trust. By thanking God for what He has already done and for what He will do, we are reminded that His plans are perfect, even when they don't align with our immediate desires. Life is full of moments where we don't understand the "why" behind our struggles, but prayer invites us to trust in God's timing and purpose. When we choose to focus on gratitude, we align our hearts with God's will, and this enables us to see His blessings, even in the most difficult circumstances.

Moreover, offering prayers of gratitude cultivates spiritual resilience. When we make a habit of thanking God, we become more aware of the daily blessings He bestows upon us the strength to get through tough days, the comfort of His presence in times of uncertainty, the provision He grants in unexpected ways. Gratitude helps us recognize that even the smallest blessings are evidence of God's love and care.

In doing so, we develop a heart posture that can face challenges with grace and strength, knowing that God is always at work behind the scenes.

In the act of continuous prayer, we begin to understand that God's goodness isn't dependent on our circumstances. Even when things seem unclear, when the road ahead feels uncertain, or when we are faced with trials, we are called to praise God, knowing that He is faithful. Prayer invites us to rest in this knowledge, trusting that God's plans for us are for our ultimate good (Jeremiah 29:11). And it is through this gratitude that we find the peace that surpasses understanding, peace that calms our hearts and guides our steps, no matter the season of life we are in.

So, whether in times of joy or in moments of trial, let us always come before God with hearts full of gratitude.

Through prayer, we are not only asking for His guidance but also praising Him for who He is and what He has already done. Even when we don't see the big picture, we trust that God is weaving everything together for His perfect plan. Let us remain steadfast in prayer, continually lifting up our gratitude, knowing that He hears us and walks with us through every season of life.

Prayers
Grateful for Health and Strength:

Heavenly Father, I come before You with a heart full of gratitude for the health and strength You have provided. Thank You for the energy to care for my loved ones and the resilience to face each new day. I am grateful for the moments of wellness and healing that You have granted us.

Help me to continue caring for my body and soul, knowing that my strength comes from You.

In Jesus' name I pray, Amen.

Grateful for Support and Community:

Lord, I am so thankful for the support system You have placed around me. Whether it's family, friends, or fellow caregivers, I feel Your love through their encouragement and help. Thank You for the people who lift me up and the community that surrounds me with kindness and understanding. May I never take these relationships for granted.

In Jesus' name I pray, Amen.

Grateful for Peace in the Chaos:

Father, I thank You for the moments of peace amidst the chaos. Even in the busiest of days, You provide quiet moments to reflect and reconnect with Your presence. I am grateful for the calm that comes from knowing You are in control, and for the peace that surpasses all understanding.
Help me to find and appreciate these moments every day.

In Jesus' name I pray, Amen.

Grateful for Growth through Challenges:

God, I thank You for the growth and lessons learned through the challenges I face. Each struggle brings me closer to You and teaches me resilience, patience, and trust. I am grateful that even in difficult times, You are molding me into a stronger and more compassionate person.

Thank You for walking with me through every trial.

In Jesus' name I pray, Amen.

Grateful for Small Victories:

Lord, thank You for the small victories in my caregiving journey. Whether it's a good day for my loved one or the completion of a task that once seemed overwhelming, I know these moments are Your blessings. Help me to recognize and celebrate these victories, no matter how small, and to always remember that Your hand is guiding me through.

In Jesus' name I pray, Amen.

Overwhelm:

Heavenly Father, I come before You feeling overwhelmed by the weight of caregiving. The responsibilities seem too great, and my strength feels small. Please grant me peace in the midst of this storm, reminding me that I do not walk this path alone. Calm my anxious heart, and help me release these burdens into Your hands, knowing You will carry me through. Strengthen my spirit and give me wisdom to face each day with courage and clarity.

In Jesus' name I pray, Amen.

Guilt:

Lord, sometimes I feel guilty for not doing enough or not being able to be everything my loved one needs. But I know that You see my heart and my efforts. Help me release this guilt, knowing that I am doing my best and that You will fill in where I fall short. Remind me that my worth is not measured by perfection, but by the love I give. Guide me to care for myself, so I can care for others with renewed strength.

In Jesus' name I pray, Amen.

Anxiety:

Lord Jesus, I am often filled with anxiety about the future and the unknowns that caregiving brings. Calm my restless mind and replace my fears with the assurance of Your presence. Help me trust in Your plan, knowing that You are in control of every situation.

Lead me to a place of peace where I can focus on today and let go of my worries for tomorrow. Strengthen my faith, so I can rely on You fully in each moment.

In Jesus' name I pray, Amen.

Isolation:

Father God, in this journey, I sometimes feel so alone. Please remind me of Your ever-present companionship, even in my most solitary moments. Help me to reach out for support, to trust that there are people who care about me and want to help. Open doors to relationships and community that can surround me with love and understanding. Let me feel Your comfort in the quiet and guide me to connections that will uplift me when I feel isolated.

In Jesus' name I pray, Amen.

Helplessness:

Gracious Lord, there are moments when I feel utterly helpless, unable to improve my loved one's condition or fix what is broken. Help me to remember that my strength comes from You and that I don't need to carry this burden alone. Grant me patience in the waiting, hope in the uncertainty, and wisdom in the decisions I face. Fill me with the assurance that even when I feel helpless, You are powerful and in control.

In Jesus' name I pray, Amen.

Sadness or Grief:

Lord of comfort, my heart feels heavy with sadness and grief for the loss I am experiencing. Help me to process these feelings without being consumed by them. Remind me of the hope I have in You, even in difficult times. Fill me with Your peace that surpasses understanding and help me to find moments of joy in the midst of sorrow. Thank You for walking with me through every valley.

In Jesus' name I pray, Amen.

Inadequacy:

Father, I often feel inadequate for the demands placed upon me as a caregiver. Strengthen me in my weakness and remind me that I am enough because You are with me. Equip me with the knowledge, patience, and endurance I need, and help me trust that I am doing the best I can with Your guidance. Fill me with the confidence to step forward in faith, knowing that You will provide for every need.

In Jesus' name I pray, Amen.

Anger or Frustration:

Lord, I confess that I sometimes feel anger or frustration during this caregiving journey. Please calm my spirit and help me respond with patience and grace. Show me how to manage these emotions in a way that honors You and my loved one. Let me remember the love that brought me into this role and the strength You offer when my patience runs thin. Help me to forgive myself and others, and to move forward with peace.

In Jesus' name I pray, Amen.

Depression:

Heavenly Father, I feel a deep sadness that weighs heavy on my soul. Lift me out of this darkness and help me see the light of hope that You bring. Surround me with people who can offer encouragement and remind me to listen and that I am not alone in this struggle. Guide me to care for my own mental health and to seek help when needed. Restore my joy and help me find purpose even on difficult days.

In Jesus' name I pray, Amen.

Resentment:

Lord,there are moments when resentment creeps into my heart, resentment for the sacrifices, the time, and the challenges. Forgive me, and help me release these feelings, knowing that caregiving is an act of love. Grant me a spirit of gratitude for the opportunity to serve and replace resentment with compassion and grace. Teach me to find balance and joy in the service I give and help me remember why I began this journey.

In Jesus' name I pray, Amen.

Emotional Detachment:

Father, I recognize that sometimes I pull away emotionally to protect myself from the pain of caregiving. Help me to stay connected with my loved one, to give my heart fully while also protecting it with healthy boundaries. Teach me how to love deeply without being overwhelmed and show me how to be present even in difficult moments. Renew my spirit and my emotional energy, so that I can care with compassion.

In Jesus' name I pray, Amen.

Loss of Identity:

Father, in the midst of caregiving, I sometimes lose sight of who I am outside of this role. Please help me rediscover my own identity, passions, and purpose. Show me how to balance caring for others with nurturing my own soul. Remind me that I am more than this role and help me find moments to pursue my own joy and fulfillment.

In Jesus' name I pray, Amen.

Fear of Failure:

Lord, I often fear that I am not doing enough or that I will fail my loved one. Please calm my heart and remind me that I am doing my best. Help me to trust in Your guidance and release the fear that I carry. Strengthen my faith in Your plan and assure me that You will fill in where I fall short.

In Jesus' name I pray, Amen.

Resentment of Lost Freedom:

Lord, I sometimes struggle with the loss of personal freedom in this caregiving role. Help me to release these feelings of frustration and resentment and teach me to embrace the opportunity to serve. Grant me patience and joy, even when I feel restricted, and help me find small moments of freedom and joy within this journey.

In Jesus' name I pray, Amen.

Uncertainty About the Future:

Heavenly Father, I am filled with uncertainty about what the future holds for my loved one and for me. Help me to trust in Your plan and surrender my worries to You. Give me the wisdom to make decisions with clarity and remind me that You hold our future in Your hands.

In Jesus' name I pray, Amen.

Emotional Exhaustion:

Lord, there are days when I feel completely drained, emotionally and physically. The weight of caregiving is heavy, and I sometimes feel like I have nothing left to give. Please renew my strength and restore my spirit. Help me find rest in Your presence and lean on You when I am overwhelmed.

In Jesus' name I pray, Amen

Difficulty Accepting Help:

Lord, sometimes I find it hard to accept help, believing I need to do it all on my own. Please soften my heart to receive the assistance You provide through others. Help me to recognize that it's okay to lean on those who offer support and that I am not meant to carry this burden alone.

In Jesus' name I pray, Amen.

Feeling Unsupported by Family/Friends:

Father, I often feel like I'm doing this alone, without the support I need from those closest to me. Please bring me the strength to continue and surround me with a community that understands and cares. Help me to forgive when I feel let down and guide me to find encouragement in You.

In Jesus' name I pray, Amen.

Guilt Over Self-Care:

Lord, I struggle with guilt when I take time for myself, fearing it takes away from caring for my loved one. Please remind me that self-care is necessary and that I must care for myself in order to care for others. Help me release this guilt and find peace in caring for my own needs.

In Jesus' name I pray, Amen.

Loneliness:

Lord, there are times in caregiving when I feel incredibly alone. Please remind me that You are always with me and that I am never truly alone. Help me to find connection and community, even in the midst of isolation, and give me comfort through Your presence.

In Jesus' name I pray, Amen.

Checklist for the Prayer Chapter:

☐ Reflect on your emotional challenges before praying.

☐ Take a moment to quiet your mind before offering each prayer.

☐ Identify specific emotions you want to lift up in prayer.

☐ Consider how each prayer applies to your caregiving journey.

☐ Acknowledge gratitude after each prayer.

☐ Share your prayers with your support network if appropriate.

Reflection Moments:

How has prayer helped you find peace in your caregiving journey? Take a moment to reflect on the times when turning to God in prayer provided comfort and clarity. How might continuing this practice strengthen your connection to both your faith and your loved one?

Thought Questions:

- In what ways can prayer help you navigate emotional challenges as a caregiver?

- How has your connection with God been strengthened through prayer?

- Are there specific areas in caregiving where you feel a stronger need for prayer?

- How can you incorporate prayer into your daily caregiving routine?

- What emotions have surfaced during your caregiving experience?

- How has prayer provided comfort or guidance?

- After prayer, how do you feel emotionally and spiritually?

- How has your faith grown through the challenges you've faced?

- Are there any emotions not covered in the prayers of this book?

Notes:

Thoughts from the Author

As you near the end of this book, I want to take a moment to acknowledge the incredible journey you're on. Caregiving is one of the most profound expressions of love and faith, and I want to remind you that you are not walking this path alone. The caregiving journey is one filled with moments of joy, exhaustion, grief, and peace, a rollercoaster of emotions that can leave you feeling both fulfilled and weary.

I've been where you are now, and I want to thank you for entrusting me to walk alongside you through these pages. Whether you're new to caregiving or have been on this road for years, know that every step you take makes a difference. The challenges you face, the love you pour out, and the care you provide matter deeply not just to your loved one but to everyone whose life you touch along the way.

As I reflect on my own caregiving journey, I see how deeply it shaped who I am today. Caregiving for my daughter Daisy wasn't just about ensuring her physical health it was about navigating the emotional and spiritual trials that came with it. I had to dig deep to find strength when I felt empty, and it was through this experience that I grew closer to God. There were moments of despair when I felt alone, but in those moments, God's grace showed up through the kindness of friends, the support of my community, or the sheer love that kept me going.

Looking back, I realize that caregiving wasn't just a role I took on; it was a calling, and through that calling, I learned to trust in God in ways I never imagined. It was a journey of discovering how to advocate for my child, learning more than I ever thought possible, and leaning into the faith that gave me the strength to continue. My prayer life deepened, and I found that in every small victory, God was right there, guiding me through it. If there is one thing I've learned, it's that caregiving is not just about attending to the physical needs of another person, it's about nourishing the spirit, both theirs and your own. It's about the quiet moments when you hold their hand, the prayers whispered in the dark, and the faith that gives you the courage to face another day. This journey will change you, just as it changed me. You'll find parts of yourself you never knew existed, and you'll discover resilience and love in ways you never imagined. In these pages, I hope you've found both practical advice and spiritual encouragement. Whether it's managing the complexities of medical care, navigating legal and financial matters, or simply taking care of yourself, I pray that you feel equipped and empowered. But more than that, I hope you feel seen and understood. I hope you feel the presence of a community that cares for you, even if you've never met them.

Remember, this book isn't just about providing you with resources, it's about reminding you of the profound and lasting impact your care has on those around you. I hope that through this journey, you have cultivated the priceless skill of self-awareness. This awareness allows you to investigate your own thoughts and feelings, transforming challenges into opportunities for growth. Embrace this gift, and let it guide you toward becoming a forward-focused person, pressing onward through trials and tribulations. I encourage you to use this awareness to impact others, sharing your

God-given gifts to tear down walls, inspire hope, and create meaningful change in the lives of those you touch.Do you feel it? That spark of connection, of knowing you're part of something bigger, a community of caregivers who understand, who walk alongside you even in the toughest moments. You're not alone in this journey, and now you have tools, encouragement, and the knowledge that you're surrounded by others who believe in what you're doing. As you move forward, remember that you don't need to have all the answers. Lean into your faith, trust that God is guiding your steps and know that what you are doing is truly remarkable. The love you provide reflects God's love, and in that, you will always find the strength to continue. Say yes to the growth, yes to the journey, and yes to the care you so beautifully give. You've got this, and we're with you every step of the way.

With gratitude, faith, and love, Carolyn

Practical Tools for Caregivers

Caregiving brings with it a unique set of challenges, from keeping track of medications and appointments to managing daily routines and finding time for self- care. These responsibilities can feel overwhelming, especially when everything falls on you. The right tools, however, can make a world of difference, helping you stay organized and find moments of calm amidst the demands.

Tools to Help You Thrive

Caregiving requires focus, flexibility, and a lot of planning. Imagine having a toolkit designed just for you, to help streamline your day-to-day tasks, track your loved one's progress, and offer a space for you to reflect and recharge. Here's how we can help:

- Caregiver Planners: A caregiver planner can be an invaluable tool for both single caregivers and caregiving teams. For the singular caregiver, it serves as a lifeline of organization, helping you keep track of medical appointments, medications, daily care tasks, and important notes all in one place. It reduces mental clutter, allowing you to focus more on your loved one and less on trying to remember every detail. It also provides a clear record that can be shared with healthcare providers, ensuring continuity of care and preventing oversights.

- If multiple caregivers are involved, a shared planner can simplify communication and reduce the time needed to update each other. Instead of lengthy discussions on every appointment, medication change, or routine update, everything can be documented in one place. With a centralized record, each caregiver can quickly catch up on the details, and even home health nurses can use it as a reliable resource, knowing they're seeing the most up-to-date information.

- Journals: Caregiving is not just about the care you give to your loved one; it's also about the care you give to yourself. Keeping a journal allows you to reflect on your journey, process your thoughts and emotions, and explore your personal growth. It offers a safe space for you to capture your reflections, track your emotional well-being, and embrace the lessons learned along the way. Journaling can help you discover patterns, celebrate your resilience, and reconnect with the purpose that fuels your caregiving.

- In addition to personal reflections, a journal can also serve as a valuable log of events. Documenting behaviors, changes in your loved one's condition, or specific challenges provides a factual record that can be helpful for healthcare providers or serve as confirmation in unforeseen situations. While this aspect may seem daunting, it offers peace of mind, ensuring that important details are not overlooked.

- A journal is also a wonderful way to capture the sweet, funny, or meaningful moments that make this journey unique. It becomes a keepsake of memories, both joyful and challenging, that you can look back on with pride. Whether you use it for reflection, as a record, or to preserve cherished memories, your journal becomes a testament to your strength, compassion, and the love you pour into caregiving.

Reflection Moment:

Which of these tools would most help you bring order to your caregiving responsibilities? How would staying organized impact your peace of mind?

Thriving Caregiver Resources

To provide you with support beyond this book, we've developed a range of resources specifically for caregivers:

- Caregiver Planners and Journals: At *ThrivingCaregiver.com* , you can find planners and journals tailored to help caregivers like you. These resources offer practical ways to keep life organized and are designed with your specific needs in mind.
- The Thriving Caregiver YouTube Channel: Caregiving is a journey that thrives on connection and support. Our YouTube channel is in the works and is designed to be an extension of the relationship we've built through this book, a place where

you'll find valuable insights, heartfelt encouragement, and practical tools to navigate the caregiving journey. Together, we'll explore meaningful topics, share uplifting stories, and celebrate the strength it takes to care for others. Join our community and continue to thrive as a caregiver.

- Community Support and Updates: We're working on creating a dedicated space where caregivers can connect, share experiences, and access exclusive content. Follow us on Facebook and check our website for the latest updates on this supportive community.

Your Purchase Gives Back

When you invest in these tools, you're not only supporting your own caregiving journey but also helping caregivers in need through Daisy's Place, a 501(c)(3) nonprofit organization. All proceeds from our planners and journals go directly to supporting caregivers through rest and resources at Daisy's Place.

Visit *ThrivingCaregiver.com* to explore the planner, journal, and other resources that can make your caregiving journey more manageable. Together, let's create a path to stronger, more confident caregiving. *"Therefore, encourage one another and build each other up, just as in fact you are doing."*

(1 THESSALONIANS 5:11, NKJV)

By reaching out for support and using available resources, you are creating a stronger foundation for yourself and your loved one.

Prayer for Guidance in Using Resources and Tools:

Heavenly Father, thank You for providing the resources and tools that help guide me in my caregiving journey. I ask for wisdom and clarity as I navigate these aids, knowing that You have placed them in my path to lighten my load. May I use them wisely to bring comfort and care to my loved one.

Help me to embrace the support systems available, recognizing that You work through others to provide strength and direction. Lord, grant me discernment to seek and use the resources that align with Your will, and help me to be a source of support for others on this journey.

May I find peace in knowing that You are with me every step of the way, guiding me to the right tools and resources to ensure that my caregiving responsibilities are fulfilled with love and grace.

In Jesus' name I pray, Amen.

Notes:

Conclusion

May this book serve as a guide you can return to in times of need, and may you continue to find peace and strength in your role as a caregiver. Thank you for walking this journey with us. Together, we can continue to create a community of care, compassion, and hope.

Scripture Acknowledgment

www.ingramcontent.com/pod-product-compliance
Lightning Source LLC
Chambersburg PA
CBHW060154130626
46556CB00006B/2639